RIPPING THINGS TO DO

Also by Jane Brocket

The Gentle Art of Domesticity
Cherry Cake and Ginger Beer

Jane Brocket

RIPPING THINGS TO DO

HODDER &
STOUGHTON

First published in Great Britain in 2009 by Hodder & Stoughton
An Hachette UK company

Copyright © Jane Brocket 2009

The right of Jane Brocket to be identified as the Author of the Work has been
asserted by her in accordance with the Copyright, Designs and Patents Act 1988.

A CIP catalogue record for this title is available from the British Library

ISBN 978 0 340 98096 5

Typeset in MT Centaur

Printed and bound by Clays Ltd, St Ives plc

Hodder & Stoughton policy is to use papers that are natural, renewable and
recyclable products and made from wood grown in sustainable forests. The logging
and manufacturing processes are expected to conform to the environmental
regulations of the country of origin.

Hodder & Stoughton Ltd
338 Euston Road
London NW1 3BH

www.hodder.co.uk

For my family, with love

Contents

Introduction

THE JOY AND VALUE OF READING BOOKS when you are a child is twofold: first there is the pleasure of being lost in a story, and second there is the firing of the imagination that makes you want to do the things you have just been reading about. Who hasn't wanted to play Poohsticks after reading *The House at Pooh Corner*? Or jump in puddles like Alfie in *Alfie's Feet*? Or eat a russet apple while reading a book in an attic like Jo in *Little Women*? Or go blackberrying like Milly-Molly-Mandy? Or set off in a rowing boat like the Famous Five? Who hasn't, on reading a brilliant book, exclaimed 'I want to do that!'

This book is a collection of those 'I want to do that!' moments. It's a book for adults who have never forgotten what it's like to read a great story and feel impelled to re-enact it immediately, and it's a book for adults who have perhaps forgotten but are happy to be reminded. It's a book for anyone who is looking for inspiration and ideas for children's games and activities – and it's a book for children. I would hope that it also offers a starting point for many more ripping adventures because there is still plenty of buried treasure in children's books just waiting to be unearthed by avid readers.

The origins of *Ripping Things To Do* can be found in *Cherry Cake and Ginger Beer*, my previous book, which is based on the wonderful foods and treats that children in books are forever eating. In the course of my research, it became clear that not only do fictional children *eat* marvellous things they also *do* all sorts of marvellous things. They enjoy amazing adventures, learn old-fashioned skills, invent wildly imaginative games, explore their world and test themselves to the limit. They are full of ideas; they are busy, active and resourceful, and they are a huge inspiration to readers who want to do the things they do.

So what can you expect to find in here? Well, even in the very early stages of the book's development it became clear that there are two types of ripping things in children's books: those that real children can do and those that real children can't do.

Though children may dream of experiencing for themselves the freedom and independence enjoyed by characters in adventure books, they are generally unable to imitate the classic story device of absent parents. Although they may dream of it, they can't get rid of their parents for a summer (or even completely) in order to be left to their own devices in a caravan or castle or dungeon. Nor can a child normally obtain permission to go with siblings and friends on an extended sailing and camping adventure without adults, or 'help' with police investigations into local crimes, or leave home to seek treasure, all of which happens in many favourite, thrilling stories. No, I'm afraid there are some things that real boys and girls can't do, no matter how alluring or exciting the adventure, no matter how inventive, wily or enterprising the child.

This clear dividing line applies not only to patently unfeasible experiences and situations but also to the more apparently manageable activities that many children want to copy. This is best illustrated by one of my favourite William stories by Richmal Crompton, one that I kept at the back of my mind all through the writing of this book.

In 'A Busy Day' it is Christmas Day and William is delighted to receive a book entitled *Things a Boy Can Do*. He wastes no time in dismantling the library clock to make sure it is working as his new book tells him it should, which, of course, leads to him attempting (unsuccessfully) to 'mend' what was, before his investigations, a perfectly correct mechanism. After lunch he decides to borrow Cook's mincing machine so that he can follow the instructions for making a model railway signal from its various parts but finds that these are 'wrong' and need to be hammered, something his mother is unable to comprehend. The last straw is when one of the book's conjuring tricks involving an egg goes predictably and horribly wrong.

Poor William. Instead of being congratulated on his burning desire to be creative, to experiment and to entertain himself and others, he finds himself in disgrace with the rest of the household. Even the book is treated as seditious material, and when his father locks it up in the cupboard with his other confiscated treasures William complains bitterly that the book should be called *Things a Boy Can't Do*.

Mindful of this story, I realised it would be necessary to filter out the things a boy or girl can't do, and concentrate instead on including the things that can be done without loss of life, limb, fortune or valuable objects. I endeavoured to select a wide range of ideas, games and activities that are doable, affordable and within the scope of all readers. So this book plunders children's literature for all the things they *can* do, things that are practical, achievable, enjoyable, imaginative, manageable and, mostly, pretty safe. There are a few that carry an element of risk and for this I make no apology.

And where did I find these ripping things? I found them mostly in the classics; the books that have lasted longer than the generation for which they were written because they have a timeless and universal appeal.

The books I explored span a century or so, from the 1870s to the 1970s. I couldn't go back much further because even though I believe children themselves have not changed, I found that childhood, or the way that childhood is presented by adult writers, has changed out of all recognition in a century and a half. However, by the time we get to the Edwardian era, things are looking a lot more familiar, and we see the beginning of a new age of books written to entertain children and, even more daring, books that take a child's point of view. As a result, the books I select from are mostly from the twentieth century; they are books in which children are children in a way we recognise and identify with, books that influenced today's parents and grandparents so deeply.

Inevitably, though, some things had to be left out. Fantasy, science fiction, comic-strip books, most historical fiction and stories about communities of animals are not covered because I had to draw the line somewhere and, although these genres inspire many young readers' games, I decided to focus on real children in recognisable situations. And, much as I love illustrated books and books for the very young, I chose not to include them (apart from a couple of mentions) and concentrated instead on reading books for older children because they contain so much more material and creative detail to act as springboards for the imagination.

When it comes to what constitutes a 'ripping' thing, I take the word to mean 'brilliant' and 'exciting' in the widest sense possible. So, as well as the gung-ho, challenging, adventurous, physical stuff that you would expect in a book with this title, I have also included many more contemplative, thoughtful, creative things to do. This is because I think childhood is the time to acquire

the habit of enjoying 'small pleasantnesses', to borrow a phrase from Gwen Raverat's delightful childhood memoir *Period Piece*, and I like to think my book could inspire children to make paper snowflakes or spend a blissful summer's evening watching the sun set and smelling night-scented stock just as much as it might inspire boating, tree climbing and camping adventures.

The activities that made it into the book are timeless and were not chosen to be deliberately nostalgic. And even if they had been, I would make no excuses. Modern children are never short of books about children doing contemporary things that reflect the prevailing culture, but I think children need a mixed diet of influences and inspirations. They need to find out about the things children have always done, make their own literary discoveries and expand their world and imagination, and not rely on dull-witted, boring parents who have forgotten what it's like to be a child. Children need a wide window on childhood – not just a mirror that reflects their own – and books are the best way of providing this.

Many of the things to do that I suggest have been tried and tested by me, my family and my friends over the years. I have ransacked my own memory bank and the memories of others, but many of the suggestions and ideas are the result of the more recent experience of bringing up our three children.

For the last twelve years or so, we have taken our holidays in Britain, staying in places that could easily be settings for a storybook. These amazing properties are owned and cared for by the Landmark Trust (www.landmarktrust.org.uk) and include an old railway station in Staffordshire with waiting room and platform (just the place to read *The Railway Children*), a pink castle-folly on a Welsh hillside, a tall turreted tower in Sussex surrounded by a water-filled moat, a Martello tower on a Suffolk beach complete with dungeons and hammocks, and a Victorian Gothic house in Kent with a multitude of hiding places, a secret door and a lookout tower.

The buildings and locations, and the books on the shelves (all Landmark Trust properties have a good number of carefully selected titles, including children's books) have inspired some of the best-ever games and things to do. Our holidays have been filled with treasure hunts, messing about in moats, games of spying and ambush and hide-and-seek, lazing in real sailors' hammocks, playing cards, toasting marshmallows over campfires, inventing new games and, of course, plenty of reading. We have slept in Milly-Molly-Mandy-style bedrooms, re-enacted Famous Five-style adventures, played *Swallows and Amazons*-style games, enjoyed *Tom's Midnight Garden*-style nocturnal forays and *Worzel Gummidge*-style sunset-watching, and all kinds of literary feasts.

These holidays have reminded me that the world of books is a rich and varied one, and that we should make the most of the treasures it contains. We can't all live exciting, adventurous lives but we can all do exciting and adventurous things.

Jane Brocket

January 2009

Getting Started

CHILDREN NEED LOTS OF ENCOURAGEMENT and a good range of titles in order to get started with literary adventures, and there are plenty of places to begin. Any collection of children's books, old or modern, new or second-hand, is sure to yield something interesting. But for many, the best place to look is the library. It's full of books, it costs nothing, and there's the great luxury of choice.

LIBRARY ADVENTURES

I have a well-thumbed, dog-eared 1972 edition of the charming American novel *Thimble Summer* by Elizabeth Enright. It's just the kind of book I would have taken out of the library the very year it was published, when I was twelve – the kind of book that shows every sign of having been enjoyed by previous readers who have browsed the shelves in search of a good read. So it's very fitting that this book portrays going to the library as a ripping thing to do, and even a real adventure.

Citronella and Garnet are passionate about storytelling. One Saturday in the summer holidays they begin telling each other stories in their tree house but discover that even the best of best friends don't always share the same taste in tales. Says Garnet, "'You always tell stories about people that are grown up and fall in love. I like stories about children and wild animals and explorers... I know what. Let's go to town to the library and read.'"

So off they go to the local library, an idyllic-sounding, old-fashioned building set back from the road and surrounded by maples:

"Garnet loved the library; it smelled deliciously of old books and was full of stories she had never read … Citronella and Garnet poked about among the books until each one had found the one she wanted and then they settled down on a broad window seat." In no time, Garnet is thousands of miles away swimming with a seal, and Citronella is dancing in a glittering ballroom. In fact, they are so absorbed in their books that they don't realise the library has closed and they are locked in.

"But Garnet felt pleasantly excited.

'Citronella,' she said solemnly, 'this is an adventure. Things like this happen to people in books.'"

Although they fear being stuck in the library till Monday, when they are eventually rescued at around eight o'clock in the evening Garnet is a little wistful about the missed adventure; she thinks it would have been marvellous to tell their grandchildren that they had once stayed in a public library for a whole night.

PRACTICAL IDEAS FOR GETTING STARTED

➤ Browsing is a very useful skill when it comes to choosing books and one worth encouraging in a young reader as it allows for independent and serendipitous discoveries.

➤ Being let loose in a library or bookshop encourages children to develop confidence in their own tastes, and their ability to select books that appeal to them (as Garnet and Citronella do) rather than simply reading titles that are recommended/ pre-selected/ on reading lists/ 'good for you'/ 'must-reads'. There's also something very pleasant about walking sideways like a crab with your head cocked to one side, looking at the spines of books.

➤ It's a wonderful fact that you can obtain temporary visitors' tickets at any public library in the United Kingdom (proof of identity and

address is needed). This superb system means no one need ever be without literary sustenance when they are away from home.

- Make the most of your local bookseller and ask for advice and recommendations. Unsurprisingly, many of the people who work in children's sections are often well read and knowledgeable, and were great readers when they themselves were young.

- Second-hand bookshops are great places for browsing and choosing books, and children are usually very welcome. Some have excellent children's sections and you might even find a well-loved copy of *Thimble Summer* in one.

- Find out about storytelling and book-reading events in libraries and local shops. A reluctant reader may be much happier listening to a story and there's a good chance that, with time, he or she will be converted to reading.

- And finally, read, read, read to children. It's the best, the easiest and the most enjoyable way to get them into books.

10 books to read by a window in spring

Josie Smith in Spring, Magdalen Nabb (seeds and Easter eggs)

Worzel Gummidge, Barbara Euphan Todd (spring picnics and flowers)

The Railway Children, E. Nesbit (a new life)

Pollyanna, Eleanor H. Porter (spreading gladness)

The Secret Garden, Frances Hodgson Burnett (spring gardening)

The O'Sullivan Twins, Enid Blyton (Easter term at St Clare's)

Pippi Longstocking, Astrid Lindgren (refreshingly different heroine)

Coot Club, Arthur Ransome (Easter sailing lessons)

Dancing Shoes, Noel Streatfeild (primrose-picking and Simnel cake)

Five Go To Smuggler's Top, Enid Blyton (Easter adventures)

Secrets and Spies

CHILDHOOD IS FULL OF PUZZLES, which is why books about codes and clues, spies and detectives, are inordinately popular with children who are doing their utmost to make sense of the huge jigsaw puzzle of life. All the time they are growing up, children are learning how to communicate in both verbal and non-verbal ways; they watch others, log information, learn to recognise patterns, pick up clues, and do their best to put the pieces together to give answers.

Tales of mystery and espionage are as popular now as they ever have been. Indeed, the juvenile 'thriller' is one of the most reworked formats of all, and aspiring young detectives, amateur code-makers and -breakers, and special agents have a wonderful range of role models to inspire their games and teach them clever ruses and devious methods. The father of them all is Sherlock Holmes, who inspires William Brown to get out a dressing gown and wreak havoc in the name of stamping out crime, Fatty in the Five Find-Outers to carry a matchbox wherever he goes so that he can collect clues, and Jennings and Darbishire in *Jennings Goes to School* to create their own fictional supersleuth and set up a detective agency.

And if policework isn't for your children, there are still plenty of brilliant ideas for ripping things to do with codes and secret communications inspired by the classics. Contemporary titles have international spies and surveillance, and highly sophisticated technology to save the world. Although sometimes the simpler, old-fashioned methods hold good: the children in books by Arthur Ransome use semaphore and torch-flashing, while the Famous Five find heliographs work well, and Fatty uses that old spy standby, invisible ink. It seems that resourceful children will always find ways to communicate even when they are stranded, silenced or locked up in an attic.

Dressing-gown Detectives

IT WAS ONLY AFTER READING a large number of children's books in which young sleuths carry out detective work in their dressing gowns that I realised they were simply following in the footsteps of the ultimate dressing-gowned detective himself: Sherlock Holmes. Nowhere is this debt to the young detectives' idol and role model made clearer than in the William story 'The Great Detective' in *William Again* by Richmal Crompton. In this classic, William goes to see a play and is enthralled.

"... the Great Detective was the real hero of the play. He appeared (always in a dressing-gown) in his room smoking a pipe and working up clues, with his hand upon the collar of his amiable bloodhound."

William walks out in a dream. It is all so wonderful and simple:

"You just found a clue and worked it up. It would be fine to be a detective. Of course, one needed a dressing-gown and a bloodhound, but he had a dressing-gown, and though Jumble wasn't exactly a bloodhound, he was a bloodhound as much as he was any kind of a dog."

To complete the Holmesian effect, William sucks a lead pencil that represents a pipe (after first trying an actual pipe from the greenhouse: *not* recommended) and by the time he goes to bed he's determined to bring a criminal, any criminal, to justice. However, despite the fact that William is inspired by Holmes' clear thinking and dignity, he manages to conduct his own detective work in a manner that is anything but intelligent and dignified. The farce that ensues is far removed from anything you'd find in a Conan Doyle story, but I am sure it's much closer to the antics of young children everywhere

who, at some time or another, have been inspired to don a dressing gown and
thus join the ranks of Great Detectives.

 **PRACTICAL**

Once inspired by good detective/spy books children will probably find all they
need in the house for their investigations:

■→ Notepads and pens for statements and reports

■→ Paper for maps and messages (see page 17 for codes)

■→ Oranges or lemons for invisible ink (see page 22)

■→ Dictaphones, digital cameras and mobile phones for recording and
filming interviews or bugging suspects

■→ Talcum powder and soft paintbrushes for finding fingerprints

■→ Latex or rubber gloves for picking up clues

■→ Magnifying glass

■→ Torch

■→ String for tripwires and tying up criminals

■→ Dressing gowns to be worn when considering the evidence and coming
to conclusions

Cracking Codes

Dot-dot-dot-dot, dot, dash, dash, dot-dot.*

What's that tapping? And those flashes and beeps? What are the little scribbles on scraps of paper and why are those flags flapping madly? Could it be that you have intercepted a secret message sent by Biggles or the Famous Five? Are they coded communications between the Swallows and Amazons, who don't want their plans and strategies intercepted and foiled by interfering agents and adults? And how can we crack these codes and send replies?

It's easy. All anyone has to do is copy their favourite code-makers and either learn the international codes or devise their own; and if ideas are needed, look no further than *Winter Holiday* by Arthur Ransome, a book so full of codes that it's almost a code handbook.

It's the story of a group of children's snowy, arctic adventure. They make the most of an extended stay in the Lake District by mastering all sorts of signalling systems: they hang flags, employ lanterns and torches to flash signals, learn and use Morse, and devise their own signalling system with wooden halyards. They also spend hours practising semaphore or, as Nancy calls it, "scarecrow signalling" (she draws out a lovely semaphore table of little flag-flapping stick men). Her *pièce de résistance* is the message she sends to the others when she's stuck in bed with mumps and not allowed to talk to them (see page 21): what looks like a happy skating scene is actually a vital message in Morse with a sign to the North Pole, pointing west to indicate the direction in which the code should be read (right to left). So what does it say? Well, that would be telling, wouldn't it?

* 'Hello' in Morse

HOW TO SEND SECRET MESSAGES

Learn international codes such as Morse and semaphore, and the telephony phonetic alphabet used by taxi drivers and telephone operators – Alpha (A), Bravo (B) etc. – and use them in games and communications.

A	Alpha	J	Juliet	S	Sierra
B	Bravo	K	Kilo	T	Tango
C	Charlie	L	Lima	U	Uniform
D	Delta	M	Mike	V	Victor
E	Echo	N	November	W	Whiskey
F	Foxtrot	O	Oscar	X	X-ray
G	Golf	P	Papa	Y	Yankee
H	Hotel	Q	Quebec	Z	Zulu
I	India	R	Romeo		

Incorporate semaphore figures in drawings to pass on secret messages, as Nancy does (see illustration on page 21).

Practise communicating with flashing mirrors on a sunny day. Enid Blyton's Famous Five use heliographs (flashing signals made with a mirror or mirrors that reflect the sun's rays) to send messages in Morse code (short flashes for dots and long flashes for dashes) in *Five on Kirrin Island Again*.

THE SEMAPHORE ALPHABET.

MORSE CODE

A • —	**M** — —	**Y** — • — —
B — • • •	**N** — •	**Z** — — • •
C — • — •	**O** — — —	**0** — — — — —
D — • •	**P** • — — •	**1** • — — — —
E •	**Q** — — • —	**2** • • — — —
F • • — •	**R** • — •	**3** • • • — —
G — — •	**S** • • •	**4** • • • • —
H • • • •	**T** —	**5** • • • • •
I • •	**U** • • —	**6** — • • • •
J • — — —	**V** • • • —	**7** — — • • •
K — • —	**W** • — —	**8** — — — • •
L • — • •	**X** — • • —	**9** — — — — •

🌂 Or create your own code. It's very easy to make codes with letters (as anyone who has done a verbal reasoning test will know) by just writing down the alphabet and assigning a new letter to each existing letter. For example, A becomes B, and B becomes C, or A is Z, B is Y, and so on.

🌂 Or just jumble up all the letters – but make a note of which letter becomes what before you forget.

🌂 Or give numbers or symbols to each letter. You could make up themed alphabets, for example, a fruit and veg one in which A is an apple, B is a banana and Z is a zucchini.

🌂 Adapt the semaphore figures to suit your own private code and message. This gives plenty of creative possibilities: a figure with a shopping trolley, left by mum, to indicate 'I've gone shopping', or a figure kicking

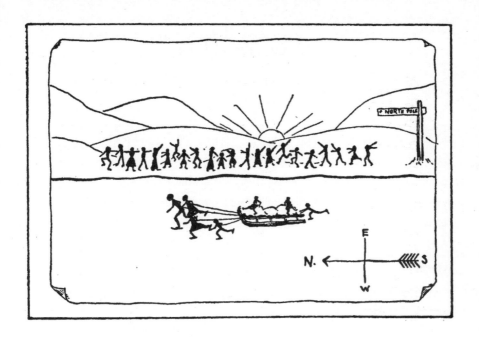

a football left on the back door to say 'I'm at the park', or a figure holding a knife and fork to say 'I'm hungry'. It's possible to tell whole picture stories this way (rather like Egyptian hieroglyphics).

Or create a more general, shared set of secret signals by agreeing and using new meanings for various symbols, flags, waves, beeps, or torch or mirror flashes.

NOTE FOR ADULTS: Remember, modern-day texting and messaging between children are just new forms of coded communication. Parents are not *meant* to understand.

Invisible Ink

ONE THING THAT MYSTIFIED me when I was young and reading thrilling tales of adventure and detection was: how do you *know* when you have received a communication written in invisible ink? And what if you send an SOS message and the recipient thinks it is just a scrap of paper and throws it away leaving you trapped, maybe for ever, in a cave or dungeon or turret? Invisible ink seemed all very well and good, but its very invisibility caused me great concern.

So I am grateful to little Bets, the youngest of Enid Blyton's Five Find-Outers and more often than not the one who makes the connection between the clues which leads to the solution of the mystery in hand, for enlightening me about invisible ink: it's the smell that tells you it's there.

Like all good amateur sleuths, the Find-Outers are keen on home-grown techniques and Fatty, a dedicated student of spy and detective books, demonstrates the effectiveness of orange juice after Bets knocks over his bottle of expensive shop-bought invisible ink in *The Mystery of the Secret Room*.

Of course, it is this very skill that gets him out of a nasty fix towards the end of the book when he needs to alert his friends to the dirty work that's going on. Out of his pocket he produces an orange (Fatty's pockets and their contents are a continual source of wonder throughout the Five Find-Outers series; "I always take tons of things about with me in my pockets, just in *case* I might need them") and he writes two messages — one visible, the other invisible — on a sheet of paper. But the children fail at first to realise the presence of the secret message (and my heart sinks at this point). Luckily Bets can detect the smell of oranges, puts two and two together, and saves her mentor.

"They smelt it. Yes, it smelt of oranges – and that could only mean one thing. Fatty had written *another* letter on the same sheet – in orange juice, for secret ink!"

Now all they have to do is pass a hot iron over the letter in order to read Fatty's *communiqué*, and off they go into the dénouement of this exciting mystery.

And the hidden message for a child to take from this story? If ever you are going to be locked up in a secret room by a gang of smugglers or crooks or thieves, make sure you have a juicy orange in your pocket.

WRITING WITH INVISIBLE INK

- Any pale liquid that oxidises and turns brown when heated is suitable for use as invisible ink. Orange juice, lemon juice, apple juice, milk and diluted honey all work well.
- Use a pen with a nib, a feather, a toothpick, a thin wooden stick, rubber stamps or simply a finger to write a message on a sheet of paper. Then leave to dry. To make the ink visible, run a hot iron over the paper.
- If you need to write two messages in one communication, use a ballpoint pen for the visible portion since anything written in ink will run when the invisible section is written. Do as Fatty does, and write one letter on the lines of the paper and one in-between the lines.
- Real spies alert readers to the presence of a secret message by using code words such as 'orange' or 'apple' in the text.

Scientific Thinking

ALTHOUGH CHILDREN SPEND THEIR LIVES asking questions, some are quite happy not to delve too deeply into the mysteries of life and the world around them, while others want more answers. The latter are dedicated observers who like to look closely and identify, collect and manage their discoveries. Like Dick in *Winter Holiday*, who is in modern parlance a 'boffin' or Fatty in the Five Find-Outers who is a 'nerd', they think scientifically.

There are also some delightful characters who make discoveries by accident, such as Pollyanna who unwittingly stumbles on the theory behind Newton's prism when she is entranced by the baby rainbows created by lampshade crystals. And there are others who, having struggled through innumerable maths/science lessons with no idea how any of what they have been taught may apply to real life, have a Eureka moment like Jennings and Darbishire in *Jennings Goes to School* when they realise maths does have some useful applications, such as accurate cake-cutting.

Unsurprisingly, books that show children thinking scientifically are often written by people who had personal interests in scientific thinking – for example, Arthur Ransome (chemistry), Enid Blyton (botany, ornithology, horticulture) and L.M. Montgomery (photography) – and they do a wonderful job of making a subject that can seem remote from everyday life when taught in the classroom come alive in the wider world. They succeed in that very difficult task of convincing children that scientific thinking is 'cool'.

How to Make a Rainbow

WHEN ELEANOR H. PORTER'S POLLYANNA encounters Sir Isaac
Newton's prism for the first time the outcome is wonderful and joyful, but not
very scientific. Pollyanna, of course, already sees the world through a lens that
breaks the world up into a huge spectrum of colour and interest, unlike most
people who struggle on most days to find even a rose-tinted lens. And when
she visits the bedridden Mr Pendleton she not only transforms his sickroom
into a rainbow-spangled grotto, she also alters his way of seeing.

Pollyanna notices the "flaming band of blue and gold and green edged with
red and violet lying across his pillow" created by the bevelled edge of a
thermometer in the window and exclaims with delight, "'Why, Mr Pendleton,
it's a baby rainbow – a real rainbow come to pay you a visit!'"

Touched by her enthusiasm for this little rainbow, and knowing that it is
made by a prism breaking light up into different colours, Mr Pendleton asks
his housekeeper to bring in a big, brass candlestick with prism pendants on an
old-fashioned candelabrum. A string is tied across the window from the sash
curtain fixtures and the twelve pendants are hooked on to it – with spectacular
results:

"It had become fairyland... everywhere were bits of dancing red and green,
violet and orange, gold and blue. The wall, the floor, and the furniture, even
the bed itself, were aflame with shimmering bits of colour."

Even Mr Pendleton is charmed, and it dawns on him that Pollyanna herself
is the "very finest prism of them all".

"'Oh but I don't show beautiful red and green and purple when the sun shines through me, Mr Pendleton!'

'Don't you?' smiled the man."

WAYS TO MAKE A RAINBOW

There are several ways of making rainbows at home.

➤ Hang old CDs on a string or washing line outdoors to create natural fairy lights.

➤ Make a lovely temporary rainbow on a sunny day with a garden hose. Use a fine spray or mist nozzle, make sure the sunlight is shining over your shoulder from behind, and hold the nozzle upwards to create a shower. There will be a wonderful rainbow in the droplets, which work as mini-prisms.

➤ Plenty of rainbow prisms are available on educational websites and in shops, or pretty crystals can be hung in sunny windows.

➤ If you can find an old pair of binoculars, take them apart and use the prisms.

➤ Create a water prism by using a clear glass or jar filled with water (a square jar or small fish tank works best). Place the container in a well-lit window in a room that is otherwise fairly dark. By moving the container around you can cause a prismatic effect on the opposite wall of the room.

➤ Place a bowl of water in a sunlit window and hold a small mirror at an angle in the water. By adjusting the mirror you should be able to create a prism on the wall.

Apply Geometry to Cake-Cutting

Children learn all sorts of survival skills at school. How to avoid games. How to eat more than one lunch. How to forge a parent's signature. How to invent a good excuse. But not many children acquire one highly underrated skill: how to cut up a cake into exactly equal portions so that everyone is happy. Yet there's always the chance they'll find themselves in a school changing-room or a dormitory with a delicious cake, a number of willing and hungry takers, and no means of sharing it fairly.

Unless they have read *Jennings Goes to School*, the first of Anthony Buckeridge's Jennings books. This wonderfully perceptive and funny book offers a brilliant solution to the problem, with a marvellous example of youthful lateral thinking and a smattering of applied mathematics.

In the run-up to his birthday and with the promise of a birthday cake from his grandmother, Jennings' sidekick, Darbishire, spends weeks compiling his cake list, adding and removing the names of his fellow pupils according to the whether or not they have been decent to him. Unfortunately, when it arrives, grandmother's cake turns out to be disappointingly tiny (six inches in diameter and one inch deep). Darbishire whittles the number on the cake list down to thirty-six, but can't work out how to divide the cake equally until Jennings comes up with the idea of applying what they have learned in maths lessons.

"They rushed off to their class-room and returned with a protractor, ruler and compass. The discovery had shattered the popular belief that mathematics was of no practical value. With the protractor laid centrally across the cake,

90°

45°

180°

9.7CM

they pricked tiny holes with the point of the compass at ten-degree intervals round the circumference."

Sadly, the boys don't actually cut the cake into ten-degree "titchy hunks" because the teachers and matron eat the cake by mistake. But all's well in the end when Mr Carter replaces the tiny cake with a much larger one (twelve inches in diameter and five inches deep) that can provide more than a few crumbs per slice.

HOW TO CUT A CAKE INTO EVEN SLICES

- Draw up a cake list several weeks before your birthday and amend as necessary.
- Request a large, circular cake with a smooth surface so that compass marks can be seen clearly.
- Have a clean ruler, protractor and compass ready.
- Use your brain or a calculator to work out the number of degrees for each piece by dividing 360 degrees by the number of slices.
- Mark out the cutting lines using the geometry kit.
- Slice carefully with a knife or long ruler.
- Serve and eat, well away from parents and teachers.

NOTES: This technique can also be applied to other circular foods, such as pizzas and puddings. A round of shortbread could have cutting lines pricked with a clean compass before baking.

Make a Star Map in Your Head

Jennings Goes to School opens with the type of address that just about every child has written at some time or other. It starts with Jennings' name and gradually moves from his school to England and Europe, to Earth, near Moon, to the Solar System, and finally to Space and More Space. Anyone who has carefully written out their own *full* address in the front of a book or diary has, like Jennings, experienced (if only fleetingly) the incredible sense of vastness and limitlessness that visions of their place in the universe evoke.

It is this wonder at the size and scale of the universe, and the stars and planets within, that captures Dick's scientific imagination in Arthur Ransome's *Winter Holiday*. Dick is a young and well-informed scientist–astronomer and is passionately interested in stars and telescopes and the wonders of the night sky. He wishes he could "keep the star map in his head" but instead has to rely on a "star-book" when he goes into the barn (his 'observatory') in the Lake District to look at stars on cold winter nights And when he knows what he is looking at, he is overawed but also empowered by what his observations and calculations of speed and light tell him:

"Those little stars must be enormous. The whole earth must be a tiny pebble in comparison. A spinning pebble, and he, on it, the astronomer, looking at flaming gigantic worlds so far away that they seemed no more than sparkling grains of dust. Distant and huge the stars might be, but he... could see them and name them and even foretell what they were going to do."

Dick is an inspiration to anyone who has ever gazed at the night sky and wished they had a star map imprinted on their mind.

⤳ PRACTICAL ⤳

A sophisticated telescope or observatory isn't essential to enjoying astronomy. Amateur astronomers often use just their eyes or a simple telescope or pair of binoculars, and are able to see the moon, various planets, stars, comets, meteor showers and eclipses.

SUGGESTIONS FOR STUDYING THE STARS

- Be a 'doorstep astronomer' (that is, stand in a doorway or on the street or in a garden) or use a bedroom window as an observatory.

- Make the most of clear nights to stargaze, if possible in a location that isn't too near the yellow lights of towns and cities which make seeing the stars more difficult.

- Start with a simple, clear star chart ('star map') that enables you to pick out the major constellations and learn their names. Dick finds the Plough, the Pole Star, Cassiopeia, the Pleiades, the Bull, the Aldebaran and Taurus with great confidence, thus inspiring readers to match and perhaps even surpass his knowledge.

- If you are not inspired by this scientific approach to astronomy, there's still plenty to be gained from more romantic and poetic stargazing. Dorothea, Dick's sister, who is as artistic and literary as he is scientific, is more taken by the idea that the Pleiades is mentioned by Tennyson and that the stars' light might have been travelling to earth since the time of Shakespeare.

- The internet is very useful for amateur astronomers and it's the best place to find monthly charts and sky maps that show exactly what's happening and when, so that you can plan your nights out.

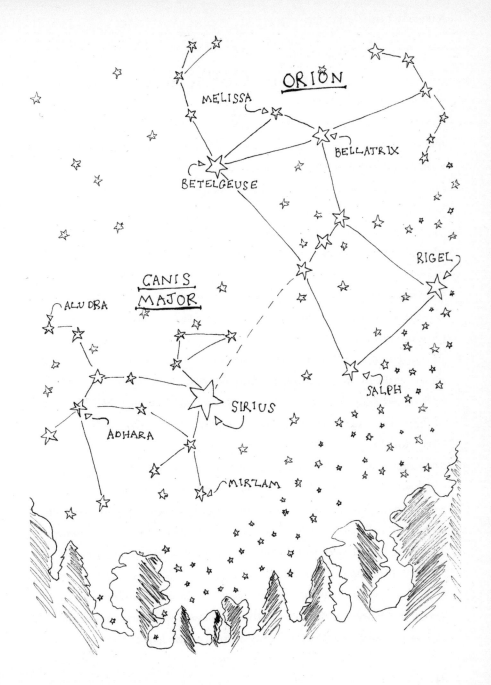

Curious Collections

CHILDREN ARE VERY CURIOUS AND AS a result they make great collectors. For them, nothing is too banal and everything has the potential to be interesting if approached with a good measure of curiosity. This explains why their magpie instincts can result in wonderfully original collections of often random, disparate things, and it also explains why they love beachcombing: it's because they never know what they are going to turn up next.

Indeed, Pippi Longstocking, the unconventional heroine of the book of the same name by Astrid Lindgren, calls herself a 'Turnupstuffer' (someone who turns up stuff when she goes looking) and suggests to her friends, Tommy and Annika, that they go 'Turnupstuffing' or searching for things. "'What kind of things?'" asks Annika. "'Oh, all kinds,' said Pippi. 'Gold nuggets and ostrich feathers and dead mice and tiny little nuts and bolts and things like that.'"

Pippi is part of a great collection of literary collectors. In *Thimble Summer* Garnet and her brother Jay comb the river bed for odds and ends (clamshells, dead animals' skulls, old tobacco tins, broken teapots, bits of polished glass) which is how she comes to find the solid silver thimble that seems to bring good fortune that summer. Jennings and Darbishire spend their free time with their stamp collections – when not pretending to be detectives in Anthony Buckeridge's *Jennings Goes to School*. But the prize for the most esoteric and bizarre collections must go to Richmal Crompton's William Brown.

William organises several shows in order to raise money to buy bows and arrows and marbles. He presides as showman over a wonderful mishmash of useless but interesting gems (a fox fur stuffed to look like a bear, an exotic-looking pink-and-blue-striped white rat that has been painted with watercolours, "insecks" such as bees, beetles and butterflies, and even his snoring aunt and her teeth in a jar) in his very own version of the cabinets of curiosities or "wonder" rooms created by Renaissance men. I, for one, would be more than happy to part with a halfpenny to gain entry to this fantastic boy-collection.

PRACTICAL

Children instinctively collect what is of interest and value and meaning to them, which could be something 'worthwhile' (coins, stamps, insects, books, shells) or something apparently less so (comics, worms, soaps, feathers, beads, buttons, electrical/radio parts, marbles, football cards, sea glass, toy cars, black Lego bricks, skimming stones). But do not mock; Robert Opie has made a successful career out of collecting ephemera and it all started with his childhood collection of sweet wrappers; and Charles Darwin wrote some of his most famous books on the subjects of beetles and worms.

- Collect suitable containers to house collections or use empty drawers (like the old-fashioned collectors' drawers that were filled with beautifully arranged and labelled exhibits). Matchboxes, shoe boxes, food boxes and jewellery boxes are ideal, and can be covered with paper and labelled. Jam jars are also great for beach finds, insects and small objects.

- Keep a supply of sticky labels and tags for collectors to name and date their finds.

- One of the most popular storage places for juvenile collections is under the bed. You have been warned.

- Children could organise an exhibition of collected items for friends and family (and consider charging a nominal entrance fee as William does).

🐞 This could be held in a bedroom, spare room, a barn like William's or even outside in the garden.

🐞 Inspire budding collectors' curiosity by visiting museums with interesting collections. There are still many wonderfully old-fashioned places that bring together disparate collections and display them in traditional glass cases with carefully typed or hand-written labels. Some of the best are small, local museums that take great pride in their unusual exhibits. These are often just right for younger children because they offer plenty of curiosities but are nicely manageable.

🐞 The Natural History Museum, the Science Museum, the British Museum and the Victoria and Albert Museum in London all have unparalleled collections and enough to keep potential collectors happy for weeks. But if you are looking for something quirky the following collections are recommended.

* Moot Hall, Aldeburgh
* Pitt Rivers Museum, Oxford
* Sir John Soane's House, London
* Manchester Museum
* Kelvingrove Museum, Glasgow
* Dorset County Museum, Dorchester
* Torrington Heritage Museum, Great Torrington, Devon
* Dorking Museum

In the Kitchen

THE KITCHENS THAT FEATURE in children's books are often quite perfect. They are warm and cosy, and filled with good smells, jam jars, flowers and pets, places where something delicious is just coming out of the oven and there's someone to talk to. It's no wonder characters gravitate towards the heart of the home and gather there for sustenance, consolation and cake; and it's not at all surprising that once they are there they tend to stay a while.

There's so much children can do in a kitchen — and it doesn't always have to be cooking and baking. Kitchens with big, scrubbed, wooden tables are perfect for playing cards or writing home newspapers, but any size kitchen will do for cutting out paper dolls and snowflakes, making invisible ink or telling 'dark and stormy night' stories.

All these lovely things are described elsewhere in this book so this chapter concentrates on the fun children can have in the kitchen with food. I don't mean simply following instructions and recipes. I mean using the kitchen as a culinary laboratory for beginners. So there is inspiration from Betsy-Tacy and Tib in the Betsy-Tacy books, who make weird and wonderful concoctions with the contents of their kitchen's cupboards, and from Petie and Tom in *The Midnight Fox*, who play with combinations of foods to create a signature dish. Or maybe you need ideas for what to do with all the leftover jam jars that accumulate on shelves, or a recipe for a spot of male-bonding cooking? Or perhaps you want to gather together a band of helpers to make a superspecial celebratory birthday cake? You'll find all you need on the following pages.

And now let's get out the bowls, spatulas, scales and whisks, and have a good time in what might just be the best room of the house.

Make a Mixture

IT TURNS OUT THAT MY first youthful independent efforts in the kitchen were not as original as I'd thought. I started with the contents of the cupboards in our kitchen, a bowl and a spoon but no recipe, just a plan to make 'mixtures'. I would kneel on a stool and shake, mix, sprinkle, stir, sniff and reel, but I never dared to taste the results, unlike the far more adventurous Betsy-Tacy and Tib who make 'Everything Pudding' in *Betsy-Tacy and Tib*, the second of the series of Betsy-Tacy books by Maud Hart Lovelace, which are well known and much loved in the United States.

One snowy evening, when the three girls are left alone in Betsy's warm kitchen, they decide to teach themselves to cook. As they are not allowed to use the oven (Mamma's instructions) they use a frying pan on top of the stove, and start their 'everything' mix promisingly with bacon grease, milk, an egg and flour. Then they branch out with raisins, coffee, tea, tapioca, cornstarch and soda. It's not long before they gain confidence and add cinnamon, ginger, allspice, cloves, nutmeg (grated), salt, pepper, molasses, bay leaves, vinegar, olive oil and mustard. By now they are on a roll and in goes oatmeal, cornmeal, farina, coconut, chocolate, cocoa, butter, lard, an onion, syrup, saleratus, baking powder, rice, macaroni and citron. And then it's time for the final flourish – flavouring – because "flavoring always comes at the end". Not content with just a single flavouring, they gaily throw in *all* the available flavourings: vanilla and lemon and almond and rose.

And then, because the proof of the pudding is in the eating, they taste their mixture. With delightful understatement, they agree, "It's lovely. But we put in just a little too much of something."

✦ PRACTICAL ✦

Many children enjoy having the freedom of the kitchen and the opportunity to pretend to be a proper chef or cook or baker.

➤ Provide a stool to stand on in front of a work surface or a chair at a table, an apron, a large mixing bowl, and a wooden spoon for each child.

➤ Let them choose ingredients from the cupboards and fridge – or select the ones you are happy for them to use, for example, flour, sugar, water, milk, gravy granules, milk powder, bicarbonate of soda, icing sugar, sauces and ketchups, food flavourings and colours, rice, spices. For more ideas, look at what the girls use in their Everything Pudding (above).

➤ I find it's best to put out little bowls of ingredients plus weighing scales, sieves, spoons, forks, and spatulas, and let the children decide how to proceed. It is amazing how long these games can last and how revolting the results can be – and how much children enjoy inventing mixtures.

➤ Needless to say, this is not the time to leave them unsupervised.

INVENT A SIGNATURE DISH

Once children have mastered the basics of putting ingredients together, they can move on to more sophisticated experiments that yield edible and tasty results, like The Petie Burkis Special in *The Midnight Fox*, the excellent coming-of-age novel by Betsy Byars.

"Petie was a great eater, and he got an idea for a new food invention. It was called The Petie Burkis Special. He got his mum to make up some dough, and then on top of this dough, Petie cut up dozens of hot sausages and luncheon meats and different kinds of cheese and pickles. Then he rolled it up and baked it, and when it came out of the oven it looked like a great golden football.

Petie sliced it right down the middle with a big knife and pushed half over to me. Wonderful-smelling steam poured up into my face. We started eating and our mouths were on fire … Petie was just moaning with happiness and I ate until my stomach hurt."

Now that I have a hungry boy of my own, I recognise every detail of Petie's culinary experiment. In the boy-world, size and quantity reign supreme, any received wisdom concerning harmony of flavours and textures is ignored, making and cooking are done by eye and not by rules, and consumption of the finished dish is uninhibited and limited only by how much can be taken in.

Although this type of signature dish does seem to have a particularly masculine character, I think every young person, boy or girl, would be happy to invent one of their own. There's something wonderfully liberating about approaching a simple format – here a spherical version of a *calzone* or folded-over pizza – with a youthful spirit of improvisation and experimentation. Indeed, it wouldn't surprise me to discover that many a successful sandwich entrepreneur has started this way.

PRACTICAL

Letting children experiment with food combinations is a fine way to introduce them to basic recipe-building and making. Once they have learnt how to make something simple, cheap, sustaining, filling and reasonably balanced, you can be confident they will never let themselves go hungry when you are out or they are away from home. Below are a couple of variations on the Petie Burkis theme, but this sort of experimentation also works very well with breakfast cereals (combinations of cereals, dried fruit, nuts and seeds) and American-style muffins (use a basic recipe and adding fresh or dried fruit, flavourings, chocolate chips).

Hot bread snacks

- For a simple version of the Petie Burkis Special, heat a round loaf or large bread bun in a warm (180°C/Gas Mark 4) oven. When warmed through, slice in half horizontally, remove some of the bread, fill the cavity with a mix of ingredients and replace the top. Return to the oven and heat gently until the filling is warm and melted, like Petie's.

- Petie Burkis-style special: make a batch of bread dough (recipes on the internet or see More Bookish Adventures, page 298) or use a commercial pizza or bread mix. After kneading the dough ready for the second rising, flatten it gently into a thick circle (like a thick pizza base). When risen, scatter fillings on top as if making a pizza and roll up the dough or bring the edges up to enclose the ingredients. Bake in a hot oven (200°C/Gas Mark 6) for 20–35 minutes depending on size.

Make Danny's Marvellous Father's Marvellous Toad-in-the-Hole

"'… DAD, WOULD YOU BE ABLE to make your favourite thing of all?'

'What's that?' he asked.

'Toad-in-the hole,' I said.

'By golly!' he cried. 'That'll be the very first thing we'll make in our new oven! Toad-in-the hole! I'll make it in an enormous pan, same as my old mum, with the Yorkshire pudding very crisp and raised up in huge bubbly mountains and the sausages nestling in between the mountains!'"

Danny the Champion of the World is Roald Dahl's wonderful, heart-warming tale of a widowed father and his only son who are united against the world by a deep bond of love and affection. They live a bohemian life in a gipsy caravan, eat windfall apples, cook a very limited range of dishes on a single paraffin burner and are idyllically happy until outside agencies and busybodies start to interfere.

By the end of the tale, though, Danny's father realises it's time they had a proper oven in which to roast food such as pork and lamb and beef and, of course, pheasant. But it is the much homelier comfort food – toad-in-the-hole – that they decide to make first, a dish which brings back memories of warm kitchens and a mother's home-cooking.

Toad-in-the-hole is probably the ultimate in male-bonding food; it's a laughably, self-consciously macho dish which depends for full effect on pantomimic proportions of whopping sausages and magically rising batter. It has everything needed to please and entertain and satisfy anyone with a boyish sense of humour and is a great recipe for dads and lads (or, indeed, any other family combination) to make together. And it's clearly just the thing for a great British caravan holiday.

 **PRACTICAL**

This is the recipe we use and it gives a generous ratio of batter to sausage. It uses comically fat pork sausages, but you can use whatever type of sausage you prefer. And as for the gravy, well, I would guess that Danny and his marvellous dad wouldn't turn their noses up at Bisto or instant gravy in their gipsy caravan, but home-made onion gravy is very delicious if you have the time and inclination to make it.

TOAD-IN-THE-HOLE

Serves 6

> *340 g plain flour*
> *½ teaspoon salt*
> *3 eggs*
> *900 ml milk*
> *2–3 sausages per person (or according to taste and appetite)*
> *2 tablespoons beef dripping or lard for frying the sausages (or 3–4 tablespoons mild olive oil or vegetable oil)*
> *1 large roasting tin or 2 smaller tins*

1. Preheat the oven to 220°C/Gas Mark 7.
2. First make the batter. Sift the flour and salt into a large mixing bowl. Make a well in the centre and crack the eggs into it. Beat with a whisk, gradually

incorporating the milk until you have a smooth liquid. Leave to stand while you get the sausages ready.

3. Heat half the fat or oil in a large frying pan and brown the sausages for 5 minutes. Remove the sausages with a slotted spoon and put on a plate until needed.

4. Pour the leftover hot fat or oil into the roasting tin(s), add the rest of the fat or oil, and heat in the oven for a few minutes until smoking hot.

5. Remove the tin(s) from the oven, pour in the batter and arrange the sausages in the batter.

6. Return the tin(s) to the oven and cook until puffed up and browned. This will take 30–35 minutes for the smaller tins and up to 45 minutes for the large tin.

7. Serve immediately with gravy.

Jam Jars

TIME WAS WHEN EVERYONE had a stash of jam jars in the larder or scullery, in the kitchen or on a shed shelf because it was unthinkable to throw them out. After all, they had so many uses, and mums or dads or aunties or neighbours would always be able to produce an empty jam jar for any given situation.

I admit I still collect jam jars knowing that they *will* come in useful. But sometimes I need to be reminded of all the uses they can be put to and I was pleased to find plenty of inspiration in children's literature. With so many characters eating jam in books (it seems to have played an integral part in the lives of British children for most of the twentieth century), it's not surprising that empty jam jars appear so often.

RIPPING THINGS TO DO WITH JAM JARS

- Use large jam jars filled with home-grown roses as the centrepiece to a special birthday-tea spread like the one prepared for Perks in E. Nesbit's *The Railway Children*.
- Make a room pretty and homely by arranging little bunches of simple flowers in jam jars, as Kathleen does in E. Nesbit's *The Enchanted Castle*. She uses marigolds, but nasturtiums (see page 130) also look lovely.
- Make your own butter in a jam jar. Just half-fill it with milk, close the lid tightly and shake the jar madly until the milk separates and turns into butter and whey.

Jam jars are indispensable on fishing trips. Make a classic container for water, tiddlers and tadpoles by tying string round the neck to create a handle. As used by My Naughty Little Sister in 'Going Fishing' by Dorothy Edwards and by Milly-Molly-Mandy and Billy Blunt in Joyce Lankester Brisley's 'Milly-Molly-Mandy Goes on an Expedition'.

Use a jam jar as a hand-warming container for hot stew on a spring picnic like the one John and Susan enjoy in *Worzel Gummidge* by Barbara Euphan Todd. Ladle hot casserole or stew into the jar and wrap it in hay, a tea towel, small bath towel, or in an old jumper, and put inside a picnic bag – the stew will stay hot if well insulated.

Fill jam jars with coloured sand and sell them to make money. In *Betsy-Tacy*, Betsy and Tacy some sand and create colourful layers and stripes in jars, which they sell to family, friends and neighbours.

Refill with jam. Go blackberrying for the fruit or to a pick-your-own farm. Or grow a pumpkin and make pumpkin and ginger jam as Milly-Molly-Mandy does in 'Milly-Molly-Mandy and the Surprise Plant'.

Making Stuff

I THOUGHT LONG AND HARD about the title of this chapter before deciding that the word 'stuff' is the right one because children adore making 'stuff'. They don't have to sit down with a plan or an objective; they simply enjoy making and creating, adding, layering and playing with materials and textures. If the end result is something useful or beautiful, that's a bonus. The most important thing is the process, the doing and the making, the having a go, and keeping an open mind about the outcome. This is just what My Naughty Little Sister does when she takes up knitting or cuts out pictures from magazines, and she demonstrates beautifully the joy of waiting and seeing where stuff takes you.

Other children, though, like to have more of plan, like the Fossils in *Ballet Shoes* when they make paper chains to decorate the house at Christmas or Milly-Molly-Mandy when she cuts out paper dolls. And then there are the children who like to have a project that can develop according to supplies and whims until it becomes a thing of beauty; a Milly-Molly-Mandy-style patchwork tea cosy that requires lots of little pieces of fabric satisfies a child's magpie instinct as much as it does the desire to make something, and a Borrowers'-style doll's house could involve weeks and months of pleasurable, fiddly, rewarding activity.

The best way for children to get started is to read the stories and have plenty of basic stuff-making stuff to hand. Old-fashioned things like pencils, paints, crayons, paper, cardboard, scissors and glue are still the best. Add some sparkle and glitter, fabric, felt, yarn and thread, and a helping hand, and it won't be long before your stuff-makers begin to resemble some of the most creative, happy and absorbed children in literature.

Make a Borrower's House

IT'S NOT SURPRISING THAT SO many children are fascinated by *The Borrowers* and their kingdom beneath the floorboards. It's a miniature parallel universe, but of the most imaginative, topsy-turvy kind, and it's all done with a lively spirit of improvisation; something that will be recognised by anyone who has used spoons to dig soil, string as intravenous drips, tinfoil for masks, and masking tape for pretend leg-waxing.

Mary Norton's details are wonderful. Walls are papered with old letters, stamps become regal portraits, chests of drawers are fashioned from matchboxes, cotton reels are used as stools and coins are plates. Fuel is kept in a mustard box and shovelled on to the fire with a mustard spoon, and the chimney is an inverted brass funnel. Homily knits cotton thread on sewing pins or darning needles, while Pod uses a hat pin as his climbing stick when he goes out on borrowing expeditions. The rooms are carpeted with blotting paper (ideal because it was "warm and cosy and soaked up spills"), and the Borrowers' luxurious bath is a small tureen which once held *pâté de foie gras*. Best of all is Arrietty's bedroom, made out of two cigar boxes; when she lies in bed she can look up at a wonderfully glamorous ceiling picture of painted ladies in Havana.

This ingenious, small-scale, recycled world is a marvellous source of inspiration for a child to make one of their own. It doesn't have to be for dolls or trolls, either. Toy soldiers, small stuffed toys, model animals, cars, Playmobil characters and Lego people all need good-quality housing. The best place to start is the book itself, then it's just a matter of being imaginative. The real challenge is to do as the Borrowers do. Borrow and recycle; don't buy.

꧁ PRACTICAL ꧂

There are no hard and fast rules for creating a version of a Borrowers' house, but it's probably best to use a container or series of containers that can be moved if necessary and kept in a safe place. A drawer is perfect as it makes a lovely single-storey dwelling which can be tidied away in an instant, and young hands can easily reach into it without knocking everything over. There is also something very intriguing for the doll's house-maker about having a bird's-eye view of the universe they are creating and controlling (one of the reasons I never liked shop-bought dolls' houses with their restricted access and views).

Alternatively, sturdy cardboard shoe boxes can be used; shoe shops will usually give them away if asked. One box may be enough, or an empire can be built up, if desired, by gluing or taping 'rooms' together and cutting interlocking doors. It's worth keeping the box lids so that the boxes can be stacked, and the contents kept safe, when the doll's house is not in use.

Before children starting to decorate and furnish the house, it's a good idea for them to emulate Pod and go on a borrowing expedition. You never know what might turn out to be useful and beautiful, or have an alternative use in a Borrowers-inspired house.

USEFUL THINGS FOR MAKING A BORROWER'S HOUSE

→ Scraps of material and felt for bedding, curtains, covering furniture, rugs and carpets.

→ Small packs of tissues or rolls of cotton wool for beds and settees (cover them with fabric).

→ Matchboxes, soap boxes and small food boxes are ideal for drawers, kitchen units, fridges, baths.

→ Pipe cleaners, beads, buttons, toothpicks, cocktail sticks, tinfoil, bits of old jewellery, used cotton reels, tiny containers, safety pins, chess pieces and pincushions have all sorts of hitherto undiscovered uses — for example, pipe cleaners could be used as table legs or picture frames.

→ Buttons, coins, bottle tops for plates and bowls.

→ Magazine pictures and stamps for wallpaper, pictures and portraits.

→ Include bought pieces such as a doll's house, Playmobil, Lego, Barbie, MyScene, Polly Pocket figures, furnishing and accessories.

→ Have glue, stapler and staples, scissors, paper clips, Sellotape, pencils and colour pens to hand.

Milly-Molly-Mandy's Paper Dolls

DO YOU REMEMBER MAKING CHAINS of paper dolls? All the figures neatly lined up, all sweetly holding hands, like naive versions of regimented soldiers or high-kicking Tiller girls? And the moment when you'd finished cutting them out and, hoping to goodness you'd not severed their arms, you could exclaim 'ta da!' as you unfolded your concertina.

I loved creating paper dolls, and would spend ages colouring them in and deciding whether they were identical or non-identical sextuplets or octuplets (as the sister of twins, I was fascinated by multiple births, and as the mother of twins, I still am). As with all paper crafts which involve clever folding and cutting, such as origami and paper-cutting, there is an element of magic in the process. Even simple paper-doll chains work in a seemingly mysterious way.

When Milly-Molly-Mandy's teacher is staying with the family, and is taught how to make hot cakes by mother, in return she shows Milly-Molly-Mandy how to make sailor dolls. For this story in *The Adventures of Milly-Molly-Mandy*, Joyce Lankester Brisley, clearly understanding that many young readers would like to make their own versions, thoughtfully provides a lovely illustration of how it's done. There's really nothing more to it.

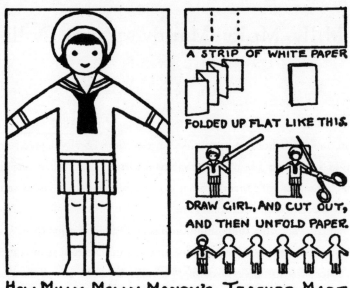

A STRIP OF WHITE PAPER

FOLDED UP FLAT LIKE THIS.

DRAW GIRL, AND CUT OUT,
AND THEN UNFOLD PAPER.

How Milly-Molly-Mandy's Teacher Made
Little Sailor-Girls.

HOW TO MAKE PAPER DOLLS

➡ It's best to use medium-weight paper or light card. Flimsy paper will tear easily and the figures won't stay upright. Having said that, you can experiment and make large and extended paper-doll chains with sheets of newspaper if you want to create a different effect.

➡ Gather pens, pencils and scissors to create and cut out the designs.

➡ Colour in with crayons, markers, colouring pencils and, if you wish to go further, dress and decorate the dolls with paper, buttons, wool, sequins, glitter, scraps of fabrics and glue.

➡ There's no need to stop at doll figures. There is nothing to prevent a creative cutter making terraces of houses, birds on wires, rows of flowers, trees, cars and much more.

Make Pauline, Petrova and Posy-Style Paper Rings

IN MANY WAYS, IT'S THE LOVELY ILLUSTRATION by Ruth Gervis on page 57 rather than the words in *Ballet Shoes* that makes paper chains (or paper 'rings' as Noel Streatfeild calls them) look so appealing. The drawing is a sweet reminder of all the times in childhood spent licking and gluing and stapling strips of paper together to decorate the house in time for Christmas. It's just the kind of simple, repetitive activity children need after a long, busy term at school. How lovely to be like Pauline, Petrova and Posy and sit around a table with paper and glitter and stamps and inks and staplers and pots of glue, enjoying warmth and companionship, and the chance to make something pretty.

Paper chains don't have to be just for Christmas, though. They can brighten up rooms for parties and special occasions and they look pretty festooning bedrooms.

PRACTICAL

It's now possible to find all kinds of ready-to-make paper chains such as gummed or peel-and-stick versions on patterned, plain or metallic paper. It's far more interesting, though, to have creative and unusual paper chains made from recycled or hand-decorated paper.

IDEAS FOR MAKING PAPER CHAINS

- The size of the strips can vary depending on the desired effect: tight chains that look like caterpillars, long, languid, droopy chains, or the traditional garland effect.
- When cutting, create a different effect by using pinking shears or special paper scissors that give unusual wavy or patterned edges.
- Recycle paper: wallpaper, magazines, sturdy wrapping paper, old books and maps all make unusual paper chains. An old atlas made into a paper chain would be a great way of 'uniting' the world, and the lines on these and Ordnance Survey maps also make useful straight cutting lines.
- Use floral paper to make a lei.
- Designer paper: use craft, printer or brown paper. Colour in, paint, stamp or potato-print the paper and cut it into strips. Alternatively, pre-cut the strips and stamp or print each one. Or decorate the paper with glitter or glitter glue (think swirls, lines, criss-crosses, dots and spots).
- Use paper glue, Sellotape or a stapler to secure each link.
- Stop when you've filled the house with paper chains, or have run out of paper or steam.

My Naughty Little Sister's Guide to Cutting Out

FOR EVERY ANGELIC CHILD IN LITERATURE there is a mischievous one, so when My Naughty Little Sister takes up her scissors and card in 'My Naughty Little Sister Cuts Out' by Dorothy Edwards, the outcome is very different to Milly-Molly-Mandy's neat paper dolls (see page 53).

My Naughty Little Sister has a cold brought on by overzealous splashing in puddles and waterlogged wellington boots, and she is fidgety, bored and not tempted by the button box or a picture book. But she does like the sound of her mother's suggestion to create a scrapbook with a "big book with clean pages", old cards and glue, and "nice snippy scissors from Mother's work-box". She cuts out her images "and then she laughed and laughed". In a somewhat demonic way, it turns out.

"She laughed because she had stuck them all in the book in a funny way. She stuck the lady in first, and then she put the basket of roses on the lady's head, and the cow on top of that, and then she put the house and the squirrel under the lady's feet. My naughty little sister thought that the lady looked very funny with the basket of flowers and the cow on her head."

Her collage is wonderfully surreal, and similar in concept to the Monty Python visuals and the work of artists such as Salvador Dalí. Her playful, topsy-turvy vision is wonderful, and no doubt many children left to their own devices would soon leave the straight and narrow path of everything in its rightful place to experiment with surrealism.

Once rules have been broken, though, the problem is knowing when to

stop. After her scrapbooking adventures, My Naughty Little Sister goes on a scissor-and-glue bender, wrecks the table top, cards and newspapers, attempts to snip the cat and finally cuts up a parcel containing fabric for her bridesmaid's dress. The young reader is in turns horrified and secretly thrilled, and any adult reading is keenly reminded of the need to stay close by when a child is armed with scissors and has a knowing smile on his/her face.

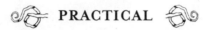

PRACTICAL

Children can have plenty of straightforward or surreal fun cutting up old cards before it all goes pear-shaped.

- Collect and/or recycle birthday, Christmas and greetings cards, postcards, magazines, comics, catalogues, old illustrated picture books.
- Glue sticks are the least messy option, although many children love using PVA glue in a pot, and brushes or plastic spreaders.
- Children's paper scissors are the safest means of cutting (and are useless on fabric).
- A scrapbook can be bought or one can be made from sheets of plain or craft paper that can be stapled together between covers made from thicker paper or card.
- Cover the work or table surface with newspaper. Spread out the cards and pictures, set out paper/book and glue. Stand back and let the children create. Use the Dorothy Edwards story if you need to make suggestions for pictures.
- Stop the activity before sharp scissors and sticking glue are applied to clothing/furniture/curtains/pets.

Bring Back the Scrap Bag

I DO HOPE THE JOY OF FABRIC scraps is not a thing of the past. A box or bag or drawer filled with little pieces of gorgeous fabrics in all sorts of colours and textures is one of the most gloriously evocative and inspirational things a child can have. Just rummaging and sorting and touching and admiring can be enough to absorb his or her attention, but anyone who plays this way will eventually feel inspired to make something with the scraps.

In Joyce Lankester Brisley's 'Milly-Molly-Mandy Makes a Cosy', Milly-Molly-Mandy understands the lure of scraps and is bowled over by Miss Muggins' wonderful patchwork cosy, "a most beautiful cosy, all made of odd-shaped pieces of bright-coloured silks and velvets, with loops of coloured cord on top" and decides to make one as a surprise for Mother.

Miss Muggins, who owns the village shop, starts her off with a small piece of bright red satin. Mother lets her have scraps of green ribbon, she buys a skein of black silk with her sweet money, Grandma gives her a few black velvet offcuts, and she lets Grandpa buy her some coloured cord as a present. Aunty teaches her how to do feather stitch and gives her lavender ribbon leftovers from hat trimming, and Uncle donates his old yellow-spotted blue necktie. She learns how to piece the fabrics together and spends weeks secretly stitching in the barn.

At last the crazy patchwork cosy is ready and, when Mother turns her back to get the hot potato cakes out of the oven, Milly-Molly-Mandy quickly pops the cosy on the cocoa jug. Lots of hugging and kissing follow. "And the potato-cakes got almost cold, but the cocoa was just as hot as hot". And the reader's heart is melted completely.

PRACTICAL

It's cheap and easy to build up a useful little collection that can be turned out for children to use on quiet or rainy days.

→ Look for fabrics in markets, jumble sales, flea markets, haberdasheries and charity shops, and check the remnants boxes in department stores and fabric shops.

→ Make the most of old clothes by cutting out unworn sections – some children's clothes cut up beautifully, especially velvet party dresses, bridesmaids' dresses, shirts and cord trousers.

→ Look for treasures such as silks, satins, velvets, jacquards, lurex, metallics, tartans, ginghams, stripes, ticking, wools, cottons and anything embroidered.

→ Collect buttons, ribbons, lace and trimmings, sewing threads and leftovers of nice yarns to put in the scrap bag.

→ Crazy patchwork is a traditional way of using up scraps, but it does require certain skills such as piecing on to backing fabric and feather-stitching. Nevertheless, as Milly-Molly-Mandy demonstrates, young children can manage it if they have a measure of patience and someone to help. Crazy patchwork creates wonderfully rich and colourful results and is a great way to use up small pieces of luxurious and unusual fabrics.

→ My daughters proved that you don't have to be able to sew to make dolls' clothes from scraps. They once made a whole fashion show of outfits for their Barbie dolls using scraps and plenty of hair ties to secure the pieces of fabric (elastic bands would do, too).

NOTE: Lest you think this is all very Milly-Molly-Mandy-girly-wirly, I should point out that many boys enjoy these activities just as much as girls do. This is borne out in *Caddie Woodlawn* by Carol Ryrie Brink, which was published in 1935, long before equal opportunities, including opportunities for boys to stitch. Tomboy Caddie learns to quilt and shows off her work to Tom and Warren, who are determined to learn to be just as smart as girls with a needle.

Learn to Knit

THE DISCOVERY OF LOVELY TEXTILES and textures opens up a whole new world of colour and creativity for children. If they like the possibilities a scrap bag offers, there's a good chance they will also like knitting. Many children are fascinated by the concept and techniques of knitting and are keen to master the basics, just like My Naughty Little Sister in Dorothy Edwards' 'My Naughty Little Sister Does Knitting', who watches with great interest as her kindly next-door neighbour, Mrs Cocoa Jones, expertly wields her yarn and needles.

Mrs Cocoa Jones also bears out my belief that the best way to get knitting is to have someone show you how; preferably a kind, patient person who isn't in a rush and who is happy to unravel tangled messes and pick up dropped stitches. When she's not making cocoa, Mrs Jones is "a lady who was always knitting and knitting" so it is inevitable that one day she offers to teach My Naughty Little Sister to knit.

Lucky Little Sister, learning at the elbow of someone who gives her "odds and endsy bits of wool". She carefully knits a scarf for Mr Cocoa Jones, who is the perfect recipient of her coaly, floury, multicoloured knitting and isn't in the slightest bit worried about the holes.

"Mr Cocoa Jones said they would make nice homes for the baby moths to live in anyway, so my little sister was glad she had dropped the stitches."

What a lovely way to accept a child's quirkily knitted effort; there's more to knitting than getting it right first time, and not everyone can learn quickly. But adventures with yarn can be rewarding, soothing, creative and pleasing, knitting is a skill most definitely worth acquiring.

PRACTICAL

The very best way to teach a child to knit is by patient demonstration and supervision until he or she has mastered the basics. If you know how to knit or have a friend who can pass the skills on, skip the next couple of points.

If you don't knit and don't know anyone who does who can help, do not despair. There are plenty of how-to knitting videos on the internet. Look at YouTube and choose and follow a technique that suits you (for example, if you are left-handed or prefer to hold the needles and yarn in a certain way).

Some yarn companies and retailers arrange knitting classes for children, and hold parent and child workshops. Look at www.knitrowan.com and www.johnlewis.com for details of beginners' classes.

If you can knit but haven't done so for a long time, go to a good yarn shop and ask for a quick refresher demonstration in how to cast on, knit and purl.

Start with plain knit stitch, then introduce purl, casting on and casting off. However, there's no rush, and there are plenty of things that can be knitted with garter stitch (knitting every row) such as scarves, dish cloths, mats, little creatures, hats, squares for a knitted patchwork. There are thousands of free knitting patterns on the internet and plenty of inspirational knitting sites.

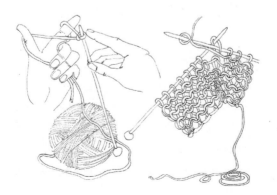

Look at www.knitty.com and www.twistcollective.com for inspiration.

Use bamboo or metal needles (not plastic) and a pure wool yarn. Cotton is beautiful but it doesn't have any 'give' and can get dirty very quickly. There are some fantastic superchunky yarns that knit up very quickly and these are excellent for older knitters (nine plus); but as they require needles they may be a little tricky for small hands. I would recommend young knitters start with aran-weight yarn on 4.5 mm or 5 mm needles, or chunky yarn on 5.5 mm or 6 mm needles.

A TEDDY BEAR'S SCARF

This is a really simple pattern for a cosy scarf to wrap round a favourite teddy bear or soft toy. It's a great mini-project for beginners because it's knitted in garter stitch (that is, knit every row) and the thick yarn ensures it grows quickly. I used 8 stitches but you could cast on 10 stitches for a wider scarf or 6 stitches for a thinner one.

To make one scarf 5cm wide and about 75 cm long you will need:

A pair of 8 mm knitting needles
One 50g ball of chunky yarn (or a yarn that has a tension of 12 stitches across and 16 rows down over a 10 × 10cm square when knitted on 8 mm needles — check the details on the ball-band)
A large, blunt-ended needle for sewing in the ends

1. Leaving a 20–25cm tail of wool, cast on 8 stitches.
2. Knit every row until the scarf is long enough to fit the intended teddy or toy.
3. Cast off evenly.
4. Sew the loose ends neatly into the scarf.
5. Add a fringe, or embellish with beads and buttons and badges if desired.

Summer Days

THE WRITERS OF CHILDREN'S BOOKS have the knack of putting into words all the things that make summer so very special when you are young – thereby making them appear even more special. By articulating the joys of the long, warm, carefree, light-filled days, they inspire readers to make the most of the never-to-be-repeated summers of youth, the summers when you can be outside from dawn till dusk like the Famous Five, or spend hours on delightful, desultory occupations such as eating a ripe, fragrant melon then making a necklace with the seeds like the Bastable children in *The Story of the Treasure Seekers* or, like Fern in *Charlotte's Web*, simply while away the days watching Charlotte spin her clever webs.

Stories set in summer also play a useful role in reminding children that this is a wonderful time to indulge all five senses, and prompt readers to notice or seek out delightful sensory experiences. Who could fail to be inspired to smell the sweet scents of a summer's evening like John and Susan in *Worzel Gummidge*? Or to decorate a plain and dowdy hat with colourful flowers like Anne of Green Gables? And would you ever be able to walk past a hedge dripping with ripe blackberries without thinking of Milly-Molly-Mandy's delicious jams and pies once you had read 'Milly-Molly-Mandy Goes Blackberrying'?

This chapter takes some of the best ideas for things to do in summer. None of them are too strenuous but all make the most of the sunshine and freedom, and have the potential to create many moments that will linger in the memory long after summer has ended. So take the time to smell the roses, laze in a hammock, and celebrate the season with carefree frolics, handstands and plenty of summer fruit.

Make a Melon-Seed Necklace

HOW MANY CHILDREN WIND DOWN in summer these days? Truly wind down to the point at which a simple, soothing, repetitive action can while away a whole sunny afternoon or warm evening? I ask this because if they aren't able or allowed to wind down, children miss out on many lovely pleasures associated with having all the time in the world, something that should be embraced and treasured as long as it lasts: the gentle contentment of sitting with friends on walls in the evenings and eating a pomegranate by picking the seeds out with pins, or lazing on the grass in the sunshine and attempting to make the longest-ever daisy chain.

I was reminded of these calm and creative activities when I read E. Nesbit's *The Story of the Treasure Seekers*. The Bastables spend a long summer holiday at home, unable to go to the seaside because money is tight, and yet they manage to find all sorts of ways of amusing themselves in the garden. They make tents, play games such as 'shipwrecked mariners', and eat coconut candy. They also club together to buy a melon for tea, "quite a big one, and only a little bit squashy at one end. It was very good, and then we washed the seeds and made things with them and with pins and cotton".

And that's all you need when you are young: a slightly squashy melon, pins, needles, cotton, and time.

HOW TO MAKE A MELON-SEED NECKLACE

- Use the seeds from any sort of melon (cantaloupe, honeydew, Galia, Charentais) except watermelon.
- Scoop out the seeds with a spoon.
- Wash the seeds in a sieve or colander to remove the pulp.
- Pat the seeds dry with a tea towel or kitchen paper, or leave them to dry in the sun on newspaper or a tea towel.
- Thread a sturdy sharp needle with a length of strong thread (upholstery thread – widely available – is best) or use a double thickness of ordinary sewing thread.
- String the melon seeds on to the string until it is long enough to pass over your head or fits around your wrist. Add beads for effect if desired.
- Knot tightly and cut the ends of the thread.
- Or why not develop the food jewellery theme and make an edible necklace?
- Make a popcorn necklace using corn popped at home (bought popcorn is too sticky) and a needle fine enough to go through the pieces of corn without breaking them.
- Make a cereal necklace with threadable honey loops, Cheerios, pretzels or any cereal with a hole in the centre.
- Sweet bracelets are an excellent party activity and treat. Fill bowls with sweets that have holes, such as Polos and Haribo, and give each child a length of elastic that will fit loosely around their wrist when knotted.

Make a Liberally Garlanded Hat

THERE'S SOMETHING UTTERLY IRRESISTIBLE about a simple hat, liberally garlanded with fresh flowers. Imagine a profusion of honeysuckle, jasmine, marigolds, forget-me-nots, roses, marguerites, foliage and blossoms entwined around the brim of a hat whose surface is barely visible. Imagine what it would be like to be the child wearing this extravagant celebration of nature and how much pleasure it would bring to her, the creator and wearer, and to any appreciative onlooker.

We live in a largely hatless age (I don't count baseball caps) and reserve our millinery for special occasions such as weddings and the races, but that doesn't mean we can't enjoy the frippery and frivolity of a floral hat when the fancy takes us, and we have only to turn to L.M. Montgomery's *Anne of Green Gables* for a lovely lesson in hat-trimming.

Anne revels in the beauty of nature all year round, and is particularly fond of flowers. So when she is denied a dress with puffed sleeves, frills and furbelows to wear to church (even though she has prayed hard for one), she sets off disconsolately, looking far too plain and sensible for her liking:

"Anne started off irreproachably … her hat was a little, flat, glossy, new sailor, the extreme plainness of which … disappointed Anne, who had permitted herself secret visions of ribbon and flowers."

But Anne, being Anne and highly sensitive to beauty, is soon distracted by a "golden frenzy of wind-stirred buttercups and a glory of wild roses" (and who wouldn't be, when they are described so beautifully?) and "promptly and liberally" garlands her hat with a "heavy wreath of them" and creates an extraordinary pink and yellow "head adornment". We have the wonderful image of Anne making up for the absence of puffed sleeves with a far more arresting accessory.

Anne is, too much of an unfettered child of nature for the locals who disapprove of her excess, but I find this makes her headwear all the more appealing. She looks like an embodiment of summer in her May Day-style hat, which is a perfect expression of her inner exuberance and her joy in nature, colours, beauty and bounty.

PRACTICAL

Trimming a hat with fresh flowers is a lovely thing to do on a summer's day. Whether it's just for the fun of it, for a party, a hat parade or a special occasion, it's quite easy to indulge in a little wild and wonderful millinery. All that's needed is a plain straw boater, some flowers and foliage, and a lack of restraint.

Cheap straw boaters are available from party shops and websites such as www.silly-jokes.co.uk and www.celebrations-party.co.uk.

- On hat-trimming day, you'll need scissors, ribbons, string, paper clips and thin wire or green, florists' wire. Sellotape also works as a quick fix.
- Gather the flowers and leaves, making sure you leave long stems that can be wound round other stems if necessary. Shrubs and climbing plants with bendy, pliable stems are ideal. Add ribbons too.
- Try winding a wreath of stems around the brim and use this to anchor your flowers. Use wire and/or paper clips to secure stems and flowers.
- Or hold your flowers and leaves in place with a firmly tied or sewn ribbon. You may wish to cover the entire hat, or just the brim.
- Wear, model and take photos.

Blackberrying

THERE IS SOMETHING IMMENSELY old-fashioned and pleasing about blackberrying. The very word conjures up so much: late-summer warmth, expeditions down country lanes or secret paths, dark berries gleaming in ancient hedgerows, battles with brambles, competitions to pick more than anyone else, stained fingers, juicy purple lipstick, and the joy of coming home laden with fruit that can be made into old-fashioned jellies or jams, tarts or crumbles. And nothing can beat the satisfaction of gathering your own food for free.

Someone who could spearhead a national marketing campaign to promote the benefits of blackberries and the joys of blackberrying is Milly-Molly-Mandy. No one else evokes the pleasure of this simple, timeless and cost-free activity as well she does in Joyce Lankester Brisley's 'Milly-Molly-Mandy Goes Blackberrying'.

When she comes home from school one day with "six great beauties" each member of her family is suitably enthusiastic about the possibilities the berries suggest. They reel off a mouth-watering list of traditional treats: blackberry puddings, blackberry jam, blackberry tart, blackberry jelly, stewed apple-and-blackberry, fresh blackberries with sugar and cream. What a litany of blackberry delights and possibilities; not surprisingly, it inspires Milly-Molly-Mandy to go blackberrying with little-friend-Susan.

A "splendid place" is found, blackberries are picked, Milly-Molly-Mandy's harvest is turned into jams, jellies, tarts and puddings, and anyone reading the story is left wanting to go blackberrying. Immediately.

PRACTICAL

The Milly-Molly-Mandy story kindly provides a good practical checklist of what's needed for a blackberry-picking expedition:

➤ "Big baskets (to hold the blackberries)
➤ Hooked sticks (to pull the brambles nearer)
➤ Stout boots (to keep the prickles off)
➤ Old frocks (lest the thorns should catch)"
➤ Or you can do as Seamus Heaney does in his wonderfully evocative poem 'Blackberry-picking' and take milk cans, pea tins and jam pots. (Pudding bowls are good containers, too). Heaney warns against leaving the fruit too long before eating; blackberry skins burst very quickly and the fruit goes mouldy in no time. So if you are going to cook or preserve blackberries, you need to have everything at the ready on the day of picking.

BLACKBERRY AND APPLE CRUMBLE

Blackberry and apple crumble is a late summer and autumn classic, and great way to make handful or two of blackberries go a long way. This recipe includes ground almonds in the crumble topping for extra flavour and texture.

Serves 6

750 g tart apples (Cox, Bramley, Granny Smith)
30 g soft brown sugar or caster sugar
400–500 g blackberries (rinsed and cleaned)

Crumble topping

    125 g butter
    150 g plain flour
    100 g soft brown sugar
    50 g ground almonds

1. Preheat the oven to 200°C/Gas Mark 6.
2. Peel, core and slice the apples. Put the slices in a large pan and scatter the sugar over them. Add a tablespoon of water and cook gently for 5 minutes or so, until the apples begin to soften.
3. Add the blackberries and stir gently to distribute them evenly before transferring the fruit to a shallow, ovenproof pie dish.

4. Make the crumble topping. In a large mixing bowl, rub the butter into the flour, sugar and ground almonds until the mixture resembles not-too-fine breadcrumbs. If you like your crumble to be crumbly rather than powdery, sprinkle a dessertspoonful of cold water over the crumble topping and lightly fork it in to make little clumps here and there, but don't overmix.

5. Now scatter the crumble over the fruit and level the surface.

6. Cook for 30–40 minutes until the top is golden-brown and the fruit juices are bubbling up around the edge.

7. Serve hot with custard or cream.

NOTE: Crumble leftovers are delicious the next day, hot or cold.

10 books to read in a hammock in summer

In the Fourth at Malory Towers, Enid Blyton (summer term at school)

Charlotte's Web, E.B. White (joys of summer on a farm)

My Family and Other Animals, Gerald Durrell (heat and insects)

Swallows and Amazons, Arthur Ransome (timeless summer activities)

The Adventures of Tom Sawyer, Mark Twain (Mississippi adventures)

The Family from One End Street, Eve Garnett (seaside picnics and river adventures)

Josie Smith in Summer, Magdalen Nabb (fishing and fêtes)

The Midnight Fox, Betsy Byars (life-changing summer holiday)

The Famous Five, Enid Blyton (idylls and adventures)

The Minnow on the Say, Philippa Pearce (treasure-seeking in a canoe)

Make a Hammock

"TWO HAMMOCKS, SIDE BY SIDE, under a huge pine tree, swung lazily to and fro in the evening breeze. In them Norah and Harry rocked happily, too comfortable, as Norah said, to talk. They had been out riding most of the day, and were happily tired. Tea had been discussed fully, and everything was exceedingly peaceful."

Hammocks are the epitome of pleasant, peaceful idleness. They invite and encourage nothing more energetic than a little gentle rocking, lounging, lazing, gazing and reading. And, as Norah and Harry demonstrate in Mary Grant Bruce's *A Little Bush Maid*, a turn-of-the century Australian classic, two hammocks next to each other are perfect for a spot of synchronised swaying on a warm and balmy evening in the bush beyond Melbourne.

I haven't yet met a child who doesn't love a hammock, particularly one in the traditional naval or 'pea pod' style. Once they've mastered the art of taking a flying leap to get into it or climbing on to stools and chairs before clambering in, a hammock can be incredibly comfortable and a wonderful place to spend hours and hours reading and rocking and swaying in the breeze.

PRACTICAL

It's simple enough to make a hammock with nothing more than some rope and a length of fabric. You will need a length of sturdy, strong fabric, for example, canvas or an old curtain, approximately 2.5 m long and at least 1 m wide, and 6 m of strong rope (climbing rope which can be bought in outdoor pursuits shops is ideal).

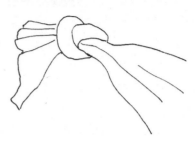

ONE

TIE A SIMPLE KNOT AT
EACH END OF THE FABRIC.

TWO

TAKE THE ROPE AND TIE A LARK'S HEAD KNOT AT BOTH ENDS.
TO DO THIS YOU NEED TO MAKE A LOOP HALFWAY ALONG THE ROPE.

PLACE THE LOOP BELOW
THE KNOT YOU'VE MADE
IN THE FABRIC

TAKE THE LOOP BEHIND
AND UNDER THE FABRIC

THREE

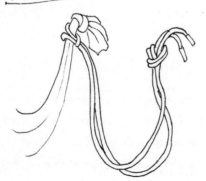

PASS EACH END OF THE
ROPE THROUGH THE LOOP
AND PULL TO TIGHTEN

TIE TOGETHER THE TWO
ENDS OF THE ROPE TO MAKE
AN EXTRA STRONG DOUBLE
ROPE TO USE TO TIE TO A
TREE OR POLE.

FOUR

TIE THE HAMMOCK TO A TREE USING A <u>FISHERMAN'S-BEND</u> OR <u>ANCHOR HITCH</u> KNOT.

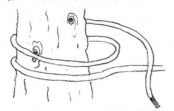 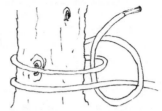

PASS THE END OF THE ROPE TWICE AROUND THE TREE.

TAKE THE ROPE AROUND THE STANDING PART AND THEN THROUGH THE LOOPS YOU HAVE JUST MADE.

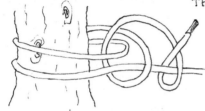 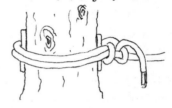

PASS THE END OF THE ROPE AROUND THE STANDING PART.

BEFORE TYING THE ROPE TIGHTLY PUT TWO PIECES OF WOOD INSIDE THE ROPE TO AVOID DAMAGING THE TRUNK.

FIVE

TEST THE HAMMOCK.

Watch a Spider Spin a Web

MANY CHILDREN IN BOOKS HAVE action-packed, adventure-filled summers in which they dash about all over the place barely pausing for breath which is, of course, why so many children whose lives are far less exciting adore reading about them. But, for children whose summers pass at a more leisurely pace, it's reassuring to know that slow and gentle is also good, because childhood is one of the few times in life when you can sit and contemplate your navel, or enjoy some lovely, slow activity such as web-weaving all day long should you wish.

E.B. White's *Charlotte's Web* teaches patience and the value of taking your time, and Fern is an excellent pupil. In the summer of the story she visits Wilbur the pig, Charlotte the spider and the other animals in the barn almost every day: "Charlotte liked to do her weaving during the late afternoon, and Fern liked to sit nearby and watch." By sitting still, and watching and observing nature, she becomes a part of it and the barn becomes a quiet, peaceful and trusting place. But Fern's mother is so worried about her going there instead of playing with other children that she confides in the doctor who replies, "How enchanting! It must be real nice and quiet down there."

His is the voice of reason; his advice is to let Fern be and, sure enough, by the time the next summer comes round, Fern thinks her behaviour was all very childish and bears out the doctor's observation that "it's amazing how children change from year to year".

Nevertheless, the book remains a delightful lesson in not rushing children into growing up but letting them do it in their own time.

Smell the Evening

"**It was too hot to go to bed** very early that night so Susan and John… were allowed to go and sit on the wall that divided the flower-garden from a little paddock. The farmer had told them that they would see the moon rise there. It was very still … A mixture of scent rose up from the sweet jumble of flowers at the foot of the wall – cherry pie, sweet briar and the night-scented stock that always reminded Susan of tiny butterflies.

'The moon rose slowly and in such a fiery glow that they wondered for a minute or two whether the sun had made a mistake and was getting up at the wrong time."

As adults, we tend too often to overlook many of the small pleasures that life offers us, like the one Susan and John enjoy in Barbara Euphan Todd's *Worzel Gummidge*. We are so bound up with bedtimes and routines and hours of sleep that it's easy to forget the sheer magic of a warm evening after a hot summer's day. How many of us remember being a child and lying wide awake in a stuffy, light-filled bedroom, completely unable to go to sleep – and wondering at the meanness of adults who wouldn't let us out to revel in the balmy air, the stillness of twilight, the evening smells, the setting of the sun and the rising of the moon.

Although this might strike some adults and older children as the sort of thing Fotherington-Thomas, the famous poetic sissy ("hello clouds, hello sky") at St Custard's in the Molesworth books by Geoffrey Willans and Ronald Searle would enjoy, there is no doubt that experiencing a summer evening is a wonderful thing to do. How could anyone, young or old, not be captivated and awed by the sight of a huge golden moon rising in the darkening sky or by the spectacle of a red and gold and orange sky as the sun sets? And if you throw in the delicious smells of night-scented flowers, it's a quite intoxicating mix.

PRACTICAL

The summer holidays are the best time for the special treat of staying up late to enjoy nature's evening performance. We once had a holiday on the west coast of Scotland and promised the children the fun one evening of driving further west to sit on a beach and watch the sun set with a big box of Maltesers. For various reasons we never quite did it, but the idea became so fixed in the children's minds that they have since negotiated many a sunset-watching, chocolate-munching evening on the basis of making up for lost time.

➤ There are just a few prerequisites for an evening of watching the moon rise: a clear sky, a good vantage point such as a wall, beach, deckchair or terrace, a west-facing position (best of all, a west coast) and as large a moon as possible (check current phases of the moon in the newspaper or on the internet).

➤ For lovely night scents, grow or seek out night-scented stock (*Matthiola bicornis*), evening primrose, tobacco plant (*nicotiana*), sweet rocket (*Hesperis matronalis*), mock orange (*philadelphus*), honeysuckle, sweet briar, oriental lilies, heliotrope ('cherry pie') or border phlox (*Phlox paniculata*). Plant them under a window, in a window box or near a back door just for the pleasure of sniffing them in the evening.

Bed in Summer

In winter I get up at night
And dress by yellow candle-light.
In summer, quite the other way,
I have to go to bed by day.

I have to go to bed and see
The birds still hopping on the tree,
Or hear the grown-up people's feet
Still going past me in the street.

And does it not seem hard to you,
When all the sky is clear and blue,
And I should like so much to play,
To have to go to bed by day?

From *A Child's Garden of Verses*
Robert Louis Stevenson (1885)

Have a Stone-Spitting Competition

NO, I KNOW IT'S NOT LADYLIKE. Yes, I know it's not gentlemanly, either. But even Enid Blyton could see how much fun it is to see how far you can spit fruit stones – as long as you are well away from polite society. And just to prove it, she allows the impeccably brought-up Dick to indulge in a damson stone-spitting contest in *Five Fall Into Adventure* with a *girl* – but makes sure he does so when they are hidden behind rocks on a beach. (Even tomboy George is astonished and shocked at his behaviour and Anne thinks he's quite dreadful.)

But this doesn't stop the unknown 'ragamuffin' girl and Dick (who quickly reminds George that they did the same thing with cherry stones the year before) from going head-to-head to see who can spit stones the furthest; the girl, Jo, is the winner by a clear margin of at least three feet and gains an ice cream and Dick's admiration:

"Nobody's ever beaten me before like that, not even Stevens, a boy at school with a most enormous mouth."

PRACTICAL

➡ Lazy summer days in the countryside, on the beach, by a river or in a garden are perfect for a little uncouth stone-spitting.

➡ Use biodegradable fruit leftovers such as cherry stones, damson stones or plum stones.

➡ Eat the fresh fruit, gather your stones, sit in a straight line, set a target if desired, then spit and compare distances.

➡ Develop your technique. Jo's winning way is to put a stone in her mouth, take a deep breath and spit out (making sure she doesn't inhale the stone), but I have found that most children naturally have a good idea of what to do.

➡ Buy an ice cream for the winner.

➡ Buy ice creams for everyone else (this is what the well-behaved Dick does).

➡ If Enid Blyton were writing today, she'd make sure Dick and Jo do the correct thing and pick up their spat-out stones and put them in a waste bin or bag. Quite right, too.

Trees

CAN YOU ENVISAGE A WORLD without trees? How soulless, how flat, how un-magical it would be? Imagine being a child and not being able to clamber up from branch to branch, looking for the best footholds, and nooks and places to sit and dangle your feet while watching the world go by, like Milly-Molly-Mandy. Or not being able to host an impromptu tree party like Pippi Longstocking with buns and coffee flying everywhere. Or not being able to find the best spot for a simple (or sophisticated) tree house where you can have Secret Seven-style meetings or *Thimble Summer*-style storytelling sessions with your best friend. Imagine not having the joy of reaching up or leaning over and picking a plum or pear or apple and biting into it there and then, as so many children in books do. If we didn't have trees, how would children make old-fashioned toys like bows and arrows, kites and popguns? Where would they find the perfect stick on which to roast a pig's tail or a marshmallow? Or kindling for the campfires on which they are cooking them?

It's all quite unthinkable, which is why many of the best, most evocative and most in-touch-with-real-children books contain significant trees: trees with special characters and attributes, trees that offer refuge and solace or excitement and adventure, trees that inspire readers to look again with new eyes at the trees around them. And if you don't have a tree of your own, you could grow one in a bottle like My Naughty Little Sister.

Climb a Tree

TOM'S "FIRST INTEREST IN A GARDEN ... was tree-climbing. He always remembered his first tree in this garden – one of the yews round the lawn. He had never climbed a yew before, and was inclined to think ever afterwards that yews were the best."

It may (or, for the many who did the same when they were young, it may not) surprise adults to discover that aside from the intrepid Tom in *Tom's Midnight Garden*, a great many ace tree climbers in children's books are girls. There is Hatty building a tree house with Tom, and there is Pippi Longstocking hosting tree parties, and Pollyanna using the tree outside her bedroom as an alternative to the house stairs, and Milly-Molly-Mandy finding herself stranded on a high branch when the ladder she has used is removed, and Bessie and Fanny shinning up the magic faraway tree in search of new lands, and Betsy and Tacy in *Betsy-Tacy* climbing a tree together to seek a very private place where they can share the sadness of a bereavement.

The urge to scramble and clamber up trees comes to these children, boys and girls alike, as naturally as breathing. They wouldn't think of *not* climbing an eminently climbable tree if they found one. After all, isn't that one of the main reasons trees are there? To be conquered, like Mount Everest? So that climbers can find out what really is at the top?

It is this that makes Enid Blyton's *Magic Faraway Tree* stories so compelling; the top of a tree, like the end of a rainbow, is one of those elusive places that is mostly unattainable and therefore perfect for fantasy, wonder and

imaginings. It is the potential conquerabilty that makes tree-climbing heroic *and* romantic, and as appealing to girls as boys.

Tree-climbing is one of the great freedoms left to children, and I am adamant that fearful adults and the safety police should not take it away from them. Children love testing their nerve and physical skill, and tree-climbing is a wonderful way to do it. So let them go. Let them climb trees and experience one of the great, unmissable thrills of life.

Build a Tree House

WRITING ABOUT JUST ONE OF THE tree houses in children's books is difficult because there are so many that inspire, and each one captures the excitement and the thrill children feel when they have a private space that adults can't reach, where they can't be overheard, and where they and their friends can twitter away like birds high above the rest of the world.

There's Garnet's house in an oak tree in Elizabeth Enright's *Thimble Summer* with a ladder to reach the platform where she and her friend, Citronella, come to eat lunch and tell stories. There's the tree house Hatty works so hard on in *Tom's Midnight Garden* by Philippa Pearce; the house that is extra-special because it's hers and nobody else's and the best hiding place ever. And then there's Milly-Molly-Mandy's magical little nest, in Joyce Lankester Brisley's *The Adventures of Milly-Molly-Mandy*, in the hollow of an oak tree, with floorboards made by her uncle and furnished with a wooden box table, cushions, a rug and even a vase full of flowers. Here she hosts a tea party for her friends – milk to drink and bread and jam and gingerbread to eat, which all sounds perfectly wonderful.

But for me the best tree house of all is the one in Enid Blyton's *Well Done, Secret Seven* and it achieves this accolade because the children make it themselves, thus provoking pangs of envy and internal cries of 'I want to do that!' in every reader. How exciting it would be to be one of their club, to make a splendid meeting place with "boards and boxes and cushions, and make a little store-place for biscuits and drinks and books and things". To be with them when they go looking for suitable trees with low-down branches so that they can

A. SIMPLE PLATFORM
B. CUSHIONS AND BLANKETS
C. ENTERTAINMENT
D. TREE CANOPY
E. TRAP DOOR
F. ROPE LADDER
G. PULLEY FOR FOOD AND DRINK

climb up and down easily. To join in the fun of tying boards to branches and to experience the satisfaction of creating your very own tree house.

"I bet nobody ever had so much fun making a tree-house before!" That's what George said, and I'm willing to bet she is right, but I'll also bet that many other children might enjoy making a tree house just as much after they've read *Well Done, Secret Seven*.

A SIMPLE TREE HOUSE

Building a tree house can be a challenging but enjoyable collaborative project for children if there is a suitably wide and sturdy tree available and at least a couple of stronger, older children (or adults) who can heave planks of wood up into a tree and secure them safely with rope. However, if this type of tree house is not possible, then there is a wonderful alternative, which has the added advantage of not even requiring a tree.

A platform tree house like the one pictured would be simple and straightforward with the help of a DIY enthusiast or friendly carpenter. It can be erected under a tree, or built in the corner of a garden or next to a wall. If the platform is 1.8 m or so off the ground it feels high, but isn't actually dangerously high, and if you are worried about children falling off, a fence can be built around the edge.

The platform is on four or six stilts, and access is via a trapdoor and/or rope ladder. A roof can be built to give shelter and a few optional extras added to make the tree house more exciting. A rope swing could be tied from a sturdy branch, and a pulley set up on another so that food, drink and other essential supplies can be delivered with ease. The latter is also useful for adults who wish to use the tree house after the children have gone to bed; the bucket makes a fine ice bucket for a bottle of wine.

Pippi's Tree Party

ACCORDING TO PIPPI, THE HEROINE of Astrid Lindgren's *Pippi Longstocking*, a tree is also a perfect location for an impromptu party. Pippi's garden is full of old scented roses, fruit trees and "best of all – several oak and elm trees that were perfect for climbing". Having invited the more reticent Tommy and Annika to scramble up the tree, Pippi declares it's the ideal spot to drink coffee and off she runs to her kitchen, returning with coffee and home-made buns.

As it's impossible for Pippi to do anything in a conventional way, she tosses the coffee cups up to the others from her position on the ground like a juggler in a circus "but sometimes it was the oak that caught them, and two coffee

cups broke... Then it was the rolls' turn, and for a long time there was a shower of rolls in the air. At least they didn't break".

Pippi then climbs up with coffee pot and cream and sugar (this is a very refined tree party) and when the threesome have finished eating and drinking, she simply throws the cups down on to the grass "to see if the china they make these days is very sturdy". I may not encourage my own children to do the same, but there is a lot to be said for Pippi's desire for empirical knowledge. She is never happy to simply accept facts from anyone – not even adults – and feels duty bound to test them in the same way she tests all the accepted rules of childhood. It would be a very hard-hearted reader who didn't take vicarious delight in her youthful anarchy and mayhem.

PRACTICAL

Who wouldn't want to emulate Pippi and have a tree party? All that is needed is food, drink, a suitable tree and some basic juggling skills (even Pippi's aren't always that good).

IDEAS FOR A PIPPI-STYLE TREE PARTY

➤ If crockery is going to be juggled it's best if it's unbreakable.
➤ An alternative method of getting food and drink up the tree is to use a bucket-and-string pulley system over a branch.
➤ Food suggestions: oranges, apples, plums, muffins, bread rolls, plain sponge cakes and Swedish cinnamon rolls are all eminently jugglable. Parents may baulk at the idea of children drinking hot coffee or tea in trees (Annika spills some coffee on herself but decides it doesn't matter) so cold drinks may be more suitable.

Pick Your Own Fruit

"IT IS THE MOST MARVELLOUS THING to be able to go out and help yourself to your own apples whenever you feel like it. You can do this only in the autumn of course, when the fruit is ripe, but all the same, how many families are so lucky? ... Our apples were called Cox's Orange Pippins, and I liked the sound of the name almost as much as I liked the apples."

In Roald Dahl's *Danny the Champion of the World* Danny has an interesting, cash-strapped, bohemian lifestyle with his widowed but very marvellous dad, and he fully appreciates and enjoys the fact that he can simply stretch out and pick a deliciously ripe piece of fruit straight from a tree above their gipsy caravan. In many ways, what Danny has is the ultimate pick-your-own experience.

It's ironic that this type of fruit-picking experience has become something of a luxury or a special treat for many children these days. Which is a shame, because picking ripe fruit is something very special, something absolutely of a perfect summer moment, and something every child, ordinary or bohemian, should experience.

PRACTICAL

There are several ways of picking your own fruit: grow it, pick it for free from friends' or neighbours' trees, or go to a 'pick your own' farm

➡ Older neighbours, friends and family members may be happy to let children pick fruit rather than see it go to waste, if they are unable to pick it themselves or need help doing so.

➡ There are now more than a thousand pick-your-own farms in the United Kingdom; google 'pick your own farms' to find one near you. It's a great family activity and the freshly picked fruit always tastes extra-delicious.

➡ Alternatively just one or two fruit trees in a garden can provide enough pickings for a family, and allow for the luxury of eating ripe fruit straight from their branches. Choose fruits that everyone likes such as plums, apples or pears.

➡→ Even if you are short of space, it's possible to grow small bushes of fruit like redcurrants, blackcurrants and gooseberries in pots. Strawberries are particularly good for growing in pots and window boxes because the fruit can hang over the sides to ripen without the risk of being eaten by slugs or affected by rot – and children love picking the ripe ones as they appear.

GROWING STRAWBERRIES IN POTS

- Buy strawberry plants ('Aromel' and 'Cambridge Favourite') from garden centres in mid-spring or raise from seed, if you prefer, and plant in 25 cm-wide plant pots (terracotta looks nice, but plastic works just as well).
- Put a layer of gravel or broken crocks in the base of each pot, then fill the pot with multipurpose potting compost.
- Make a hole for the strawberry plant, which should sit level with the surface of the compost (not above it), and water in well.
- Keep the strawberry pots in a light, sunny position and water frequently, especially in dry spells. Pick the strawberries as they ripen.
- Discard the plants after a maximum of four years.

Grow a Bottle-Tree

NOW HERE'S A RIPPING THING for little children to do: grow an acorn in a bottle to make a 'bottle-tree'. This is inspired by one of Dorothy Edwards' delightful My Naughty Little Sister stories, which are full of timeless activities for four- and five-year-olds.

When My Naughty Little Sister finds a shiny, brown acorn she decides she wants to plant it. Unfortunately, her father isn't amenable to having his best border dug up, but her sweet, naive plan is rescued by her more understanding mother, who gently shows her how to grow the acorn indoors in water. Knowing the reader will also be intrigued, Dorothy Edwards offers a basic but useful biology lesson for budding botanists.

"Shall I tell you how she did it, in case you want to try?"

You can almost hear the chorus of 'yeses' as Mother takes her narrow-necked bottle and fills it with water.

"Well now, my naughty little sister put the pointy end of the acorn into the water, and left the bottom of the acorn sticking out of the top – (the bottom end, you know, is the end that sits in the little cup when it's on the tree).

'Now,' said my mother, 'you can watch its little root grow in the water.'"

In time, the little root begins to grow and a shoot appears and, incredibly excitingly, two tiny baby leaves. At this point My Naughty Little Sister announces that "we will plant it in the park, just where there are no trees, so it can grow and grow and spread and spread into a big tree". So she plants it carefully all by herself and the plan works; we find out at the end of the story that her oak tree has outgrown her.

HOW TO GROW AN ACORN IN A BOTTLE

➤ Acorns are ripe when they fall from the tree and their caps come away easily. Collect them in autumn on country walks or from local trees in parks, streets or gardens.

➤ Use a narrow-necked clear glass bottle so that the roots are fully visible. My Naughty Little Sister probably used something like an old-fashioned sterilised milk bottle, but today you need to look for a clear glass cordial bottle or wine bottle.

➤ Follow Dorothy Edwards' instructions and keep the water level topped up.

➤ Once you have a shoot, it's up to you whether you plant the seed out or throw it away. A compromise is to plant it outdoors in a large pot so that its growth can be observed. Don't plant trees in parks, open spaces or woodland without first checking whether restrictions apply.

It's possible to grow other tree seeds, such as conkers from horse chestnut trees and sycamore 'helicopters', in outdoor pots of compost. For more details, see www.bbc.co.uk/gardening/gardening_with_children/homegrownprojects_trees.html

Make a Popgun

FOR CENTURIES, CHILDREN KNEW HOW to make their own toys using
whatever was available in the home or provided by nature. In the days before
plastic and Toys 'R' Us, all sorts of brilliant toys were made from the twigs
and branches of common trees and shrubs. Even as recently as a generation or
two ago, you could find penknife-carrying children who made their own pea-
shooters, bows and arrows, whistles and walking sticks.

Sadly these skills are fading. Now that even conker fights are banned in
many places, there seems to be little hope for other forms of allegedly
antisocial and/or dangerous entertainment that use tree parts. So why not
buck the trend, revive ancient skills, and make a loud, noisy, fun popgun like
the one George gives Poll on her birthday in *The Peppermint Pig*?

Nina Bawden's story is set in nineteenth-century Norfolk where the locals
enjoy plenty of old-fashioned activities according to the seasons, the rhythms
of nature and the traditions of the Fens. The children arrive from a solid,
indoor suburban villa existence to experience a life that is focused on making
the most of space and the great outdoors. So there is ice-skating, tree-
climbing, hoop-chasing, mushrooming, blackberrying, a visit to an annual fair,
trips to the market, and plenty of simply living outside and amusing oneself.
They surprise themselves by adapting to, and learning to love, this new way of
life, and when George presents Poll with the home-made popgun, his
assimilation into country life is complete.

It's a perfect example of a timeless toy. It's made from "an alder stick with
the pith removed" and shoots "acorns or small balls of wet paper as

ammunition". Although wooden popguns are still popular today (they can be found in toy shops everywhere), how many children ever have a go at making their own and enjoy the satisfaction of chewing their ammunition first?

PRACTICAL

- The traditional popgun material is alder because its branches contain pith that can be removed to make a hollow tube.
- If there are no alder trees nearby, it's possible to make a popgun from other hollow materials such as plastic pipes or lengths of bamboo; use a plunger made from a wooden dowel. There are instructions on the internet (www.sciencetoymaker.org/popgun/assembl.html).

HOW TO MAKE A POPGUN

- Use a thick wooden branch, 2.5 to 4.5 cm wide, with a spongy pith centre about 6 mm in diameter. Cut a length of 15–25 cm.
- Remove the pith with heavy wire that has been hammered smooth and filed so that it can be used to poke and twist and turn and scrape out the pith, or use a skewer or long screwdriver.
- Now whittle a plunger from a solid piece of wood (a thin stick or dowel rod would also do) so that it fits inside the tube.
- Make two pellets (one for each end of the gun) by chewing small wads of paper or use berries, acorns, or pellets made from foam or cork.
- Stick a pellet firmly in each end of the tube, take the plunger and quickly push one pellet towards the other.
- You'll hear a pop as the compressed air in front of the back pellet blows out the front pellet and sends it flying.

Ripping Games

THERE'S NOT A GREAT DEAL OF MOPING in children's books; and if there is, it's usually a prelude to a tale of finding greater happiness. Even the characters who feel sad, lonely and sorry for themselves, like the three Railway Children, discover that once they begin to play games they soon cheer up. And because they have such a good time, they infect everyone with their enthusiasm and willingness to be playful. Before you can say 'jacks', the reader, too, wants to shuffle and deal the cards, get out the draughtsboard, hunt in the cupboard for an abandoned skipping rope, and throw sticks into a stream.

It seems that the very best games are either those that children have played for ever, or the ones that spring out of the moment and are made up on the spot, never to be repeated in exactly the same way. But all good games, organised or spontaneous, contain the same elements: a sense of playfulness and the ability to take what's available and invent something to do. Most ripping games are not terribly sophisticated, and the best are certainly not adult-led, but they do require energy, even if it's only to shout and argue and grab like Snubby in *The Rat-a-Tat Mystery* when he plays cards. They can be fabulously anarchic and surreal, like the game of croquet played by Alice in Wonderland, or they can be gentle like Poohsticks in *The House at Pooh Corner*. They can be wildly imaginative like the doll families created by Betsy and Tacy, sweet and very like Mary's old-fashioned skipping in *The Secret Garden*, or timeless and traditional like spillikins and chess.

This chapter offers plenty of ideas for ripping games gleaned from books. There are games to be played outside in the fresh air, and games that can be played indoors on wet days, in tents and on beds, by the fire or on the floor.

Play Cards

ON A COLD WINTER'S NIGHT THERE'S nothing better than staying in by the fire, dealing the cards and enjoying a long card session full of laughter and argument.

Children in books know this. In Enid Blyton's *The Rat-a-Tat Mystery* Snubby and the others enjoy a wonderful day's tobogganing before coming in for hot buttered toast and tea. They are puzzled by the mysterious disappearance of their snowman, but distract themselves by playing an imaginative version of Snap called Snap-Grab.

"They set the cork in the middle of the table and Roger dealt the cards. Whenever anyone saw that two cards were the same, he not only had to call 'Snap!' but had to grab the cork as well. This saved a great many arguments as to who had called Snap first!"

The children invite Mrs Tickle to play with them, but Snubby plays to win and grabs the cards so fiercely that he is forced to wear a glove on one hand. After a happy evening with nothing more eventful than card games and Snubby's antics, they go off to bed happy. But it's not long before Snubby is woken up by strange goings-on and he slips on his dressing gown and goes downstairs to investigate...

 **PRACTICAL**

The sheer number and variety of games that can be played with a single, compact, pocket-friendly pack of cards is staggering. Not only that, but having the odd card game up your sleeve (or in your pocket) is an invaluable social and survival skill that will help you make friends and survive boredom, journeys, illness and long winters.

Card games are great for the whole family; they cater for all ages and abilities and can be played before bed, on holiday, on rainy afternoons, in dens, cars and on trains. Adults may occasionally enjoy the simplicity of Snap, but it is worth introducing young card-players to slightly more demanding games as soon as possible. I've listed the most popular games below and given the rules for three: Snap, Cheat and Go Fish. However, there is nothing to stop anyone from modifying existing rules as Snubby, Roger and Diana do – children also enjoy inventing their own unique games even though no one is ever able to remember the rules the following day.

GOOD, TRADITIONAL CARD GAMES

- Snap
- Beggar My Neighbour

- Go Fish
- Cheat
- Old Maid

- Chase the Ace
- Patience

FOR OLDER PLAYERS

- Rummy
- Whist

- Newmarket
- Poker

- Brag

OTHER CARD GAMES

- Uno and Uno Extreme

- Top Trumps
- Happy Families

Play Olden Time Games

ONE OF THE JOYS OF READING BOOKS set in that strange and wonderful world of 'olden times' is finding out how children lived in years gone by and making the pleasant discovery that some things never change. Stories by Richmal Crompton, E. Nesbit and Frances Hodgson Burnett may not contain computers and screens and whizz-bang entertainment, but they do have details of traditional games with sticks and stones and marbles, which will never disappear simply because children will always love playing them.

One of the best 'sticks' games is spillikins, which appears in *Linnets and Valerians*, written in 1964 by Elizabeth Goudge but set in 1912. The book, like her most famous book *The Little White Horse*, has a charmingly old-fashioned style and plenty of period detail. The children get around in a horse-pulled cart, Uncle Ambrose writes with a quill and the imperious Lady Alicia commands games of spillikins played with delicate little ivory sticks – and does not expect to lose.

Spillikins is a fastidious game, not at all rambunctious or hearty; the kind of game you play with a little finger sticking out at a precious angle in the same way you might hold a fragile bone-china teacup. But spillikins (nowadays also known more prosaically as 'pick-up sticks') requires surprisingly high levels of delicacy and manual dexterity, and a quiet but determined desire to win.

The rules are minimal, bamboo or plastic versions are cheap and easy to find, and the game can be played on a flat surface anywhere. As they would most definitely *not* have said in the olden days: what's not to like?

Play Croquet Like Alice

"ALICE SOON CAME TO THE CONCLUSION that it was a very difficult game indeed."

Well, when you are knocking hedgehogs (instead of balls) with flamingos (instead of mallets) through bent-over playing cards (instead of hoops), I think anyone would find croquet difficult.

Croquet has a reputation for being a little mad (and the surreal situation Alice finds herself in is madder than ever), but maybe this is why it fascinates children. Perhaps the fact that most households do not possess a perfectly smooth, flat lawn or a set of heavy wooden mallets, leather balls and metal hoops, makes them realise that croquet is the sort of game that invites all sorts of fantastic improvisations.

Read Lewis Carrroll's *Alice's Adventures in Wonderland* with them and they'll immediately seek out walking sticks and umbrellas, find or make a sphere to act as a ball, and use legs or books to create arches. Then they are away, shouting 'Off with her head!' and turning into imperious duchesses with one swing of their 'mallets'.

PRACTICAL

If you are curious to learn the rules of the real game, go to www.toycrossing.com/croquet/play.shtml, but children are brilliant at taking the concept of croquet and altering it to suit their situation and whim.

🌂 Surreal croquet works well indoors if soft balls are used and propelled along the floor (not played golf-style).

🌂 If children want to play proper croquet outside, the Croquet Association www.croquet.org.uk sells children's and junior croquet sets, as does The Garden Game Company www.gardengame.co.uk.

🌂 One of the most memorable improvised games we have played was literary table tennis in a holiday house. The large dining table was cleared, a line of hardback books placed spine up across the middle for a net, and each player chose a small, hardback book as a bat. The only concession to real table tennis was a proper ping-pong ball. This set-up worked surprisingly well.

Play Poohsticks

I CONFESS THAT WHEN I FIRST CAME across the game of Poohsticks, my initial reaction was something along the lines of Peggy Lee's song 'Is That All There Is?'

Poohsticks is the game invented by Winnie-the-Pooh in *The House at Pooh Corner* by A.A. Milne. Like Archimedes, he has a Eureka moment when he realises the fir cone he has dropped by accident into the river has reappeared on the other side of the bridge. He tests his theory that this wonderful occurrence can be repeated, then develops it by racing two fir cones against each other and keeping scores. I get the feeling that if he'd stayed there much longer he would have set up a little betting shop.

It took me a while to appreciate the subtleties of dropping a stick into a river from one side of a bridge then rushing across the bridge to watch it emerge on the other side, preferably ahead of any other sticks thrown in at the same time by other players. But as I watched my children play the game, I was drawn to the concept.

PRACTICAL

Poohsticks is a great excuse to get out into the lovely British countryside at any time of the year.

- All you need is a stream or small river, a bridge that can support all the players, and some sticks or fir cones (anything that floats and bobs on a current will work).
- Forests or woods like the Hundred Acre Wood (based on Ashdown

Forest in Sussex) are ideal; look for details of forests and woodlands on the Forestry Commission website www.forestry.gov.uk or scour Ordnance Survey maps.

HOW TO PLAY POOHSTICKS

- Check that the players begin on the side of the bridge where the water flows in and not out (that is, that they are facing upstream).
- Each player must be able to recognise his or her stick.
- All sticks should be dropped – not thrown – into the water at the same time.
- And, as Peggy Lee might have said, that is all there is.

Skipping School

A GENERATION AGO, SKIPPING ROPES were the preserve of girls in playgrounds, happily chanting counting rhymes, jumping rhythmically up and down, and running around with a rope whooshing overhead and underfoot. There may have been the occasional glimpse on television of a boxer skipping manically to lose weight before a weigh-in, but that was about it. Nowadays, however, the skipping rope seems to have vanished from the children's playground and into the adults' gym, so it's high time it was brought back. After all, as Martha's mother says in *The Secret Garden* by Francis Hodgson Burnett, a skipping rope is "the sensiblist toy a child can have".

She sends a skipping rope via Martha to the pale, weak and sad Mary who has no idea what it is. So Martha demonstrates how to skip indoors and Mary's interest is aroused. Off she goes, into the fresh air, to begin building up her puny arms and legs.

"The skipping-rope was a wonderful thing. She counted and skipped, and skipped and counted, until her cheeks were quite red."

Mary skips hither and thither, enjoying the wind and the outdoor scents, skipping round the fountain and into the kitchen garden, setting herself little challenges and laughing with pleasure until she skips right up to the robin who shows her the door to the secret garden.

Indeed, skipping unlocks the child in Mary at the same time that the key unlocks the door to the secret garden, and both are saved.

PRACTICAL

Skipping is cheap and easy, and still one of the best forms of energetic play for boys and girls.

➤ You can buy skipping ropes from toy shops or online, or alternatively children can use a length of rope or washing line.

➤ Skipping can be done by individual skippers or by groups skipping over a longer rope that is held and turned by two players, one at each end.

➤ Revisit the skipping rhymes, skipping games and skipping tricks of your childhood and pass them on.

SKIPPING RHYMES

➡ A rhyme to accompany the skipper skipping over the rope as many times as possible without missing:

> Mabel, Mabel, set the table,
> Just as fast as you are able.
> [Don't forget the salt, mustard, vinegar, pepper] *repeat faster and faster*
> *until the skipper is out*

➡ A rhyme for swinging the rope back and forth, and then over the skipper:

> Blue bells, cockle shells,
> Easy ivy over

➡ Rhymes that call in friends to skip together or take turns:

Rooms for rent, enquire within,
As I move out, let (*name*) come in.
I love coffee, I love tea.
I want (*name*) to come in with me.

I had a little puppy
His name was Tiny Tim
I put him in the bathtub, to see if he could swim
He drank up all the water, he ate up all the soap
The next thing you know he had a bubble in his throat.
In came the doctor (*person jumps in*)
In came the nurse (*person jumps in*)
In came the lady with the alligator purse (*person jumps in*)
Out went the doctor (*person jumps out*)
Out went the nurse (*person jumps out*)
Out went the lady with the alligator purse (*person jumps out*)

➡ A rhyme for skipping then running round one of the people turning the rope before rejoining:

I had a little bumper car,
Number 48,
Whizzed round the corner...
(*the jumper leaves the skipping and runs round one of the rope turners while everyone says 'corner', then rejoins the skipping*)
Slams on the brakes

Create a Doll Family

ADULTS' ILLUSTRATED MAGAZINES HAVE ALWAYS provided hours of entertainment for children like Betsy and Tacy. The pictures can be ripped out and pinned on walls, cut up and used for collages, or simply altered and doodled on. (Never underestimate the childish joy of drawing moustaches on ladies and extra body parts on men.)

The best magazine-based game I have come across is the one played by Betsy and Tacy (both aged five) in Maud Hart Lovelace's Betsy-Tacy, who each have a "doll family living in a magazine". They cut ladies and girls from their mothers' magazines and source their men and boys in men's fashion sheets, donated by the local tailor. "They cut the paper dolls from fashion magazines. They could hardly wait for their mothers' magazines to grow old." They give them names and characters, and create fabulously inventive stories and adventures. In a lovely piece of game control, they ensure that five-year-old characters always have all the best times and most beautiful names, clothes and accessories (and often go to tea with Mrs Astor and Mrs Vanderbilt) while the eight-year-olds (both girls have sisters who are eight) live plain, dowdy, unexciting lives.

What's wonderful is the way in which the dolls lie flat and lifeless within the covers until the girls settle down in their favourite, warm, cosy place next to the stove and release them, like genies, and transform them into rounded, vivacious and animated characters. This idea of a secret, private, flat-packed game, hidden between the pages of a magazine, ready and waiting to be brought to life is utterly delightful. What joy to have a game as flexible, ongoing and varied as this. How wonderful to be in charge of the fates and fortunes of an illustrated universe. And what an excellent way of recycling paper.

◦◦ PRACTICAL ◦◦

This game requires very little in way of equipment. All that is needed is:

- A cosy, comfortable place to play.
- One or more players.
- A stack of colour magazines or catalogues or old books with plenty of photos or illustrations of people and accessories that appeal to the players. It's not just for girls, either, as this game can be played with male figures and paper action-men.
- Paper scissors.
- Good names; buy or borrow a book of names. (This is a really worthwhile investment – children love using and inventing unusual and exotic names.)
- Interesting biographies for each character.
- Plenty of imagination.

Showtime

ALTHOUGH SOME CHILDREN ADORE the attention and applause that comes with performing, and devour stories about seriously stage-struck children such as *The Swish of the Curtain*, others are a little more diffident about putting themselves in the limelight. But children's books prove that you don't have to be born a star to enjoy putting on a show.

As adults we need to put aside any weary cynicism we may harbour about the jollity of putting on a show, because it is exactly this that appeals to children. There is something about being part of a company, the fun and rivalry of the joint effort, and having a great time in an innocent way, that they love. Even the shyest child can be swept along by the gang-show feel, and find something they enjoy doing (sound effects, playing a tree, shining a torch as a spotlight). We have to remember that putting on a show is all about the children having a good time and that our role as the audience is simply to watch and clap. Don't forget that the most basic shows can be huge confidence boosters, even if the performers are doing nothing more than juggling two apples or standing on their heads for five seconds.

If your children harbour secret dreams of doing the whole showtime thing for real, they should immerse themselves in Noel Streatfeild's Shoes novels, book some dancing, singing and acting lessons, and get an agent. My own taste, however, tends towards the very amateur, unintentionally funny productions, like the farcical melodramas produced and performed with a total absence of inhibition and irony by William Brown and the Outlaws, or the 'home festivals' written and performed by Meg, Jo, Beth and Amy in *Little Women*, in which they have a fine time declaiming and clashing swords, playing breathy maidens and delivering wildly overblown speeches, or the script-free version of 'Beauty and the Beast' acted by the children in *The Enchanted Castle* .

If your children aren't keen on theatrical events, there are still plenty of show-offs in books who can inspire old-fashioned talent shows: Pippi Longstocking and her circus tricks, Paddington Bear and his conjuring tricks, and Fatty in the Five Find-Outer books with his many clever disguises. This is the joy of literature. Children can find something to match their own level, whether it's dressing up for fun or treading the boards to earn a living, and books contain everything they need to know about putting on any kind of show, from the sweet and simple to the sophisticated and starry.

Let's Put on a Show!

Yes, let's! But first, let's get some brilliant ideas on how to do it from the people who put on the best shows in books. People such as the Fossils in *Ballet Shoes*, Rachel and Hilary in *Dancing Shoes*, Jerry, Jimmy and Kathleen in *The Enchanted Castle*, the March sisters in *Little Women*, and the seven children in *The Swish of the Curtain*, whose shows satisfy every stage-struck reader's hunger for glamour, greasepaint and gorgeous little details.

PRACTICAL

→ A show can be spontaneous and great fun, like the little dancing and miming show performed by Posy at Petrova's birthday picnic in Noel Streatfeild's *Ballet Shoes*, or it can fill an afternoon or several days with planning and preparing and rehearsing. This sort of extended game is an ideal activity for school holidays. In *Little Women* Louisa May Alcott points out how the March girls benefited from putting on a show: "it was an excellent drill for their memories, a harmless amusement, and employed many hours which otherwise would have been idle, lonely, or spent in less profitable society." *Plus ça change...*

→ Or, children may want to put on a more professional show, like the seven children in *The Swish of the Curtain* (was there ever a better title for a children's book about putting on a show?), written by Pamela Brown when she was fourteen and thus remarkably close in age to her readers. They find an abandoned chapel which they renovate and use as the home of their Blue Door Theatre Company. The book is pure, timeless inspiration for anyone with a passion for the performing arts.

SUGGESTIONS FOR BUDDING THEATRICAL PRODUCERS

➡ Decide what to perform. If you use a well-known plot, you can make up the words as you go along, like the children in E. Nesbit's *The Enchanted Castle* when they perform their version of 'Beauty and the Beast'. But some of the best home theatricals are the one-offs, the unique shows created by the company. Write your own play, as Richmal Crompton's William does or improvise.

➡ Once you have your story or script, you can assign roles (or hold auditions), and start rehearsing if necessary.

➡ Decide where to hold the performance. Sliding doors between two rooms are useful, and can be opened and closed easily. Or use a settee as the stage and the area behind it as the dressing room. Or use a room door as the entrance and exit.

➡ Or put on a show outdoors (think Shakespeare and the Globe Theatre). Get garden chairs out and line them up for the audience – a patio or rug could be the stage and the lawn the auditorium. Use bushes and trees as part of the scenery.

➡ Ransack the house for props. In *The Enchanted Castle* the following items are used for props and costumes: cushions, antimacassars, a clothes line, a sheepskin rug, scarves, rouge, dressing gowns, false hair, a peacock fan, a curtain tie-back, handkerchiefs, tablecloths and towels.

➡ Create costumes from whatever is available (see page 122). Think creatively and use as much sparkle and colour and splendour as possible. The March sisters demonstrate the knack of creating spectacular effects with ordinary, household items. "... Very clever were some of their productions – pasteboard guitars, antique lamps made of old-fashioned butter-boats covered with silver paper, gorgeous robes of old cotton with glittering tin spangle from a pickle factory, and armour covered with the same useful diamond-shaped bits, let in the sheets when the lids of tin preserve pots were cut."

■➔ Think about lighting and music and sound to add atmosphere. Use reading lights, free-standing lights or torches as spotlights, dimmer switches, MP3 players, CD players, and musical instruments as well as home-made sound effects.

■➔ Make (and sell) tickets to the performance(s).

PUT ON A TALENT SHOW

If acting doesn't appeal, don't give up – simply exploit whatever talent there is. Here are some suggestions:

- Sing ('concerts' can be great fun and everyone can sing a nursery rhyme)
- Dance (ballet, tap, freestyle/made-up)
- Play an instrument
- Recite poems
- Do impressions (of parents, friends, teachers, famous people)
- Gymnastics (basic forward rolls, jumps, leaps, twirls, handstands all count as gymnastics in my book – just finish with a flourish)
- Circus tricks
- Jokes and stand-up comedy
- Roller-skating – perhaps choreographed or in pairs
- Anything, really, as long as it entertains and gets a round of applause

Dressing up

NECESSITY IS THE MOTHER OF INVENTION and Richmal Crompton's William is never short of the latter. When it comes to costumes for the ambitious theatricals he likes to organise, he is frequently forced to make do with what he can purloin from his home and family – with fantastic results.

So, in 'What Delayed the Great Man' he dresses his heroine in one of his sister Ethel's silk petticoats, accessorised with a toilet-cover train, lace curtain headdress and crochet-edged towel wrap; Ginger, who plays Sir Rufus Archibald Green, sports an "Indian embroidered table-cover, with a black satin cushion pinned onto his chest, a tea cosy on his head, and an umbrella in his hand". Henry is the Hon. Lord Leopold, and wears the dining-room tablecloth and a wastepaper basket and feather on his head and William, the villain of the piece, pins a rug across his shoulder and places a black china fern pot on his own head.

The details are wonderful, the images are unforgettable, and the minute these bizarre outfits are assembled the actors step immediately into character without the slightest hint of irony or self-consciousness. But when it comes to dressing up, most children *are* like that.

 **PRACTICAL**

Many adults make the mistake of thinking dressing-up boxes should contain theatrical cast-offs, wonderfully realistic costumes and sophisticated, expensive fancy dress when in fact it's clear that imagination counts more than the actual

clothes. Like William, children see all kinds of potential in everyday garments and household items, and 'more is more' is the usual dressing-up motto.

The problem with shop-bought dressing-up clothes is that they can often only be used for one single role (Snow White, Tinkerbell, Batman, Superman) whereas something like a dressing gown can transform the wearer into a shepherd, Father Christmas, a magician, a showman, Sherlock Holmes, a bride, a beauty, Cinderella – the possibilities are endless.

Here are some suggestions for a cheap and cheerful dressing-up box.

- Dressing gowns of all types and sizes.
- Adults' clothing, such as dresses, skirts, petticoats, shirts, jackets, nighties, pyjamas.
- Shoes, especially brightly coloured high-heeled shoes, and boots.
- Old uniforms or parts thereof.
- Used bridesmaid dresses.
- Accessories such as scarves, ties, glasses, sunglasses, belts, handbags, feather boas, walking sticks, umbrellas; and hats —as many as possible.
- Anything bright, shiny, sparkly or glittery, for example, old or cheap necklaces, bracelets, clip-on earrings, or with feathers, fake fur and tassels.
- Cushions for padding.
- Cheap shop-bought tiaras, crowns, swords, wands, fairy wings, eye patches. Or make your own.

Hurrah for the Circus!

HURRAH FOR THE CIRCUS! When I first encountered Astrid Lindgren's Pippi Longstocking, she reminded me of a young, madcap circus entertainer. She is manically energetic, exuberant and eccentric, a sort of all-in-one clown/strong lady/acrobat/juggler/horse rider/tightrope walker. The more I read of her antics, the more I realised she could have just stepped out of the big top and straight into her Swedish village.

If you're still not convinced, take a look at Pippi's circus credentials. She keeps a pet monkey, bakes five hundred ginger snaps at a time, breaks eggs for baking by throwing them up in the air and catching them in a bowl (not always successfully) and is strong enough to lift a horse. Then there's the matter of her appearance, which is uncannily close to a clown's typical get-up: red hair, non-matching socks, patched dress, and shoes twice the length of her feet.

It's inevitable, then, that when Pippi goes to see a real circus she finds herself propelled by some strange force into the ring, to become the star of the entertainment, upstaging Señorita Carmencita the horse rider, Miss Elvira on tightrope and Strong Adolf, the strong man. In doing so, she inspires children everywhere to pull on some outsize shoes and run outside and join the circus.

PRACTICAL

There is a whole host of simple circus acts that can be done by almost anyone. Most don't require special equipment and are quite safe.

CIRCUS-STYLE SKILLS

All the following skills can be practised and perfected in the home circus.

- Juggling: although it's possible to buy juggling balls and beanbags, there are plenty of ordinary domestic or garden objects that can be used when learning (tennis balls, onions, oranges, bread rolls).
- Tightrope-walking: on the ground on a piece of string. Or tie a length of elastic at waist height between two points (trees, for example) and walk along it, keeping it under your feet. An umbrella can be used to aid balance – and for effect.
- Clowning: water fights (with hosepipes, water guns or empty washing-up liquid bottles), silly string, helium balloons, balloon-tying. It's also good fun to do clown-style make-up with face paints.
- Acrobatics: cartwheels, somersaults, handstands, walking on hands, headstands, leapfrog.
- Bicycle tricks: wheelies, monocycles.
- Strong man: lifting people, objects, pets. Or pretending to.
- Dressing the part: tights, tutus, swimming costumes and trunks, fairy wings, wands.
- Stilt-walking, balancing, human pyramids, trampolining, mime, magic tricks.

SEE A REAL CIRCUS

The best place to look for details of permanent and touring circuses is www.circus-uk.co.uk.

Make an ('Ugly-Wuglies') Audience

THE BIGGEST PROBLEM FACING ANYONE who puts on a show is how to bring in the punters. How many budding thespians have hung up their wigs and disconsolately turned their backs on the acting profession because no one came to see them perform? How many potential Laurence Oliviers and Judi Denches have disappeared before they could touch people's hearts because there were none present at their theatrical debuts?

What's needed is a captive audience, and there is a creative way of getting one: make your own. In *The Enchanted Castle* Gerald, Jimmy, Kathleen and Mabel decide that Mademoiselle and Eliza do not constitute a full audience, so they make seven extra members for their performance of 'Beauty and the Beast'.

"Their bodies were bolsters and rolled-up blankets, their spines were broom-handles, and their arm and leg bones were hockey sticks and umbrellas. Their shoulders were the wooden crosspieces that Mademoiselle used for keeping her jackets in shape; their hands were gloves stuffed out with handkerchiefs; and their faces were the paper masks painted in the afternoon…tied on to the round heads made of the ends of stuffed bolster-cases…

"'They look just like a real audience, don't they?' whispered Mabel."

It is a truly captive audience, or so we think. In a wonderful twist that has overtones of the story of Frankenstein's monster, this grotesque group comes alive after the play and a series of bizarre, scary adventures with the 'Ugly-Wuglies' ensues. As ever with E. Nesbit, the message is be careful what you wish for, even down to who comes to watch your plays.

PRACTICAL

The Ugly-Wuglies are a clever application of the age-old activity of making dummies. In the past (and in several of Enid Blyton's Secret Seven books) most children tried their hand at creating lifelike dummies for Hallowe'en and Guy Fawkes. But these days it's a dying art, unless you count fooling your parents into believing you are still asleep by making body-shaped humps in your bed.

Here are some suggestions for making a captive audience – everything that's necessary can be found in and around the house.

- For the structure and backbones: coat hangers, sweeping brushes, hockey and lacrosse sticks, tennis rackets, pillows, cushions.
- Body: cushions and pillows, stuffed trousers, tracksuit or pyjama bottoms, stuffed sweaters, T-shirts and jackets.
- Hands: gloves and mittens stuffed with scrunched-up newspaper, handkerchiefs or kitchen paper.
- Feet: socks, shoes, boots or wellies stuffed with rolled-up socks or scrunched-up newspaper.
- Heads: the most difficult part as they have a tendency to fall off. Stuff a small pillowcase (the type used when camping) or knitted hat. Attach to the body with safety pins.
- Faces: painted or drawn masks tied on with string or elastic, or use bought masks
- Clothing: hoodies (especially useful as they solve the head and hair problem, and can simply be stuffed and given a face), dressing gowns, belts, hats, scarves.
- Then all you need to complete the illusion is some canned laughter and pre-recorded clapping.

Dreams and Schemes

WHILE THE EXTROVERTS ARE BUSY USING every ounce of their imagination and considerable energy to put on shows and entertain others, there are plenty of introverts who prefer to channel their creativity in less obvious, more contemplative ways.

There are many attractively dreamy children in books: Anne in the Green Gables stories, Lily Ruggles in *The Family from One End Street*, Tom in *The Midnight Fox* and, my very favourite, Josie Smith who stars in the books by Magdalen Nabb. They all have the ability, often unconscious and instinctive, to think outside the confines of the present and of their everyday world. They are the ones who see and appreciate the poetry of life, its possibilities, its strangeness and beauty.

Instead of rushing and blundering headlong into life, they take it more cautiously, and take their time daydreaming, making plans and hatching schemes for the future. When things turn out well, as they do for Bobbie, Peter and Phyllis in *The Railway Children*, or the dozens of young girls in books who wish for a pony, or Mary whose secret garden flourishes, their stories also become a form of wish-fulfilment for the child who is reading.

These lovely, bittersweet stories allow their readers to think about what they dream of for themselves, how they will make the most of the world, how to face the prospect of change and growing up. Like Tom and Petie in *The Midnight Fox* making their time capsule, or Mary caring for her bulbs and plants in *The Secret Garden*, or Josie Smith sowing her nasturtium seeds, they show the reader the joys of living in the present and of thinking ahead to future moments.

Grow Nasturtiums (*Whirlybird mixed*)

NOTHING ENCAPSULATES THE MAGICAL promise of gardening better than a brightly illustrated seed packet printed with brilliant colours, lovely long flower names and arcane sowing instructions. How thrilling, how wonderful for a child is the possibility of growing something as beautiful as the picture from something as small as a seed in your own piece or pot of soil.

Josie Smith, the extremely likeable heroine of the popular Josie Smith series written by Magdalen Nabb, is someone who instinctively understands the allure of seed packets, revelling in their vocabulary, colours and possibilities, and daydreaming of neat little rows of flowers and glossy, tasty clumps of parsley. Treats are few and far between in her down-to-earth world (and seeds and seed packets fall firmly into the realm of great treats), which makes her appreciate them all the more. She is befriended by the dour, taciturn Mr Scowcroft and inspired by his gruff but clever ways of growing things in his allotment, where she first spots the seeds that fire her imagination.

"... she saw something she liked ... Seed packets. Lots of seed packets with pictures of beautiful flowers on them. Yellow flowers, orange flowers, pale blue and pink flowers, so fresh and bright that Josie Smith held her breath looking at them... 'Are you going to plant this?' She pointed to the packet of seeds she liked best of all, the orange and yellow flowers and fresh round leaves of Nasturtium (*Whirlybird mixed*)."

How appropriate that Josie Smith, always proud of her reading ability, adores every last syllable on the seed packet, and falls for the gently whimsical and evocative "Whirlybird mixed" variety which will bring a touch of magic and specialness to her wet, grey northern English town. Mr Scowcroft gives her parsley, nasturtium and snapdragon seeds in thrifty little screws of newspaper and strange instructions to "sow in drills", and with these Josie Smith enters the wonderland of growing and gardening, of dreams of beauty and bounty. In doing so, she reminds all readers of the simple joy and magic of growing something from seed. Especially Nasturtium (*Whirlybird mixed*).

◦⚏◦ PRACTICAL ⚏◦

Nasturtiums are one of the very best flowers for children to grow from seed. They are a hardy annual which means they are pretty tough, and will germinate and grow quickly and easily in the British climate. They produce beautiful, rounded leaves and stunning flowers, in a range of rich, bright colours, which can be picked and displayed in jam jars or eaten in salads. The seeds are large enough for little fingers to handle; all that's needed is just to poke a finger into the soil or compost, drop in a seed,

replace the earth, and water. Nasturtium seeds don't require a greenhouse or any extra heat to germinate, so can be sown outside and left to their own devices.

- You may also want to consider some other easy-to-grow annuals such as marigolds, sunflowers, Californian poppies, candytuft, godetia, love-in-a-mist (nigella) and cornflowers.

- Garden centres (and many of the larger supermarkets) carry a wide range of seeds in displays that make children believe they can grow anything. Alternatively, an experienced gardener (grandparent/relative/neighbour/allotment holder) may be able to share seeds and offer practical help with getting started.

- A garden isn't necessary for children to enjoy the delights of seeds. Nasturtiums and other hardy annuals can be grown in window boxes, and pots and containers filled with multipurpose potting compost. In fact, the flowers look wonderful in recycled containers such as yoghurt pots, food tins, plastic bottles and wooden boxes.

- An alternative is to do what Josie Smith does: lift a flagstone, enrich the soil beneath with compost and sow the seeds.

More Secret Gardening

IN SOME WAYS, BULBS ARE EVEN more magical than seeds. They are like buried treasure: simply hide them in the earth in autumn, leave them to get on with their secret underground life, and you are rewarded in spring with the most glorious flowers.

Mary in *The Secret Garden* by Frances Hodgson Burnett realises something wonderful is happening under the soil when she first explores the hidden garden in early spring. She finds little green shoots in the overgrown grass and weeds, and gently clears spaces for them to 'breathe' and grow. As the weather gets warmer, they become stunning snowdrops and daffodils, and clumps of orange, purple and gold crocuses that delight Mary so much she feels compelled to kiss them.

But then bulbs do this to some people, and although not everyone is moved to kiss crocuses, there is nothing to match the joy of watching the shoots and flowers emerge from the earth after a hard winter, in a burst of colour and fragrance.

PRACTICAL

Bulbs are an excellent way of starting children off with simple gardening. They need nothing more than a bag of bulbs, a patch of soil or a pot or two of compost, and a trowel (or even an old spoon) for digging little holes. They also enjoy writing the labels to put in the soil so that they can be reminded of what is growing where.

➤ Daffodils are the easiest bulbs to grow. They are unfussy and reappear and multiply year after year. Plant in September.

➤ Crocuses are also very straightforward and should be planted in September. They, too, reappear each spring.

➤ Tulips are a little fussier and most varieties don't make repeat performances after the first year. On the other hand, the flowers are stunning and the colours amazing. Plant in November.

➤ If I had to choose one beginners' bulb, it would be the hyacinth. The bulbs can be planted outside in September, but you can also buy 'prepared' bulbs for growing indoors later in the year (November/December). This means children can watch their progress even more closely, especially if the bulbs are grown in the specially designed hyacinth vases that are available from garden centres and supermarkets (often with a single bulb as part of boxed gift set) in late autumn and the run-up to Christmas. Simply place the bulb in the neck of the vase, fill with water to just below but not touching the bulb, and in no time at all the vase will be filled with a swirling mass of white roots. It's not long before a thick, green shoot appears, which eventually produces a stem with masses of sweetly scented flowers.

➤ Hyacinths are worth growing for their fragrance alone. It pervades *Tom's Midnight Garden*: for Tom, who is sent away from home to avoid measles, the hyacinths in the flower beds in the garden are powerfully evocative and their smell reminds him of his mother's indoor bulb pots at Christmas and New Year. They are the flowers he knows best, the ones whose scent convince him that the garden must be real.

➤ A lovely secret garden effect can be created with masses of bulbs – buy them in bulk at much lower prices from bulb wholesalers. Peter Nyssen (www.peternyssen.com) and Bloms Bulbs (www.blomsbulbs.com).

Make a Time Capsule

TIME CAPSULES ARE A SORT OF personal message in a bottle that you can actually rely on finding again. And although the public, *Blue Peter-* or school-organised time capsules are worthy and well meaning, they can never be as interesting as an individual time capsule put together for its maker's future interest. This is the type of capsule made by Tom and Petie in *The Midnight Fox*, the excellent coming-of-age-during-the-course-of-one-summer novel by Betsy Byars.

The story, and the time capsule within it, both emphasise how quickly children alter and how they can become almost unrecognisable to themselves year on year. At the end of the summer of change, Tom looks back and realises that "it all seemed like something that had happened to another boy instead of me. Like the time Petie and I made a time capsule out of a large jar, and we put into this jar all kinds of things, so that in a hundred years, or a thousand, someone would find this capsule, open it, and know exactly what Petie Burkis and I had been like."

As it is, they don't leave their capsule to posterity but dig it up themselves after a year and, when they look at the contents, "Petie kept saying 'I never wrote that. I know I never wrote that'... it was as if two other boys had made up the time capsule and buried it in the ground."

The boys had put in pictures of themselves and lists of things they had done, stories they had written about their families for English lessons, pictures and a poem. Petie wrote down everything he'd eaten and drunk in one day, and Tom wrote down all the books he had read in the last year. It's all intensely personal and meaningful and, for the boys, a quite amazing archaeological find even after just twelve months.

✦ PRACTICAL ✦

➤ A time capsule can be a one-off or it can be part of an Andy Warhol-style series (between 1974 and 1987 he made more than 600 cardboard-box time capsules full of now valuable ephemera). For example, there could be one for every summer of a child's life, or each New Year's Day.

SUGGESTIONS FOR TIME CAPSULES

☂ If you plan to bury the time capsule, make sure it is watertight, waterproof and non-biodegradable, for example, made out of tin or plastic or glass. Use a biscuit or cake tin and seal well, a clip-and-seal food container, or a large glass jar (a Kilner jar would work).

☂ Draw up a map to show the whereabouts of the capsule so that it can be easily located when it's time to dig it up.

☂ Alternatively, box up your items in a cardboard box, seal and label it, and ask someone to hide it for you. Make sure they make a note of where they have put it.

☂ Put in details of the name of the maker, the date of making, and fill with things that represent you at that moment to make a composite snapshot of who you are.

☂ Further suggestions include photos of family, friends and pets, lists, theatre or sports programmes, newspaper headlines, examples of favourite toys, current pin-ups, CDs of photos or home-made films.

☂ Agree a digging-up or opening date and no peeking in advance.

Wish for a Pony

AH YES, WISHING FOR A PONY. All that yearning, dreaming and longing that takes up so much time and emotional energy when one is young. No wonder there are so many pony books – the fierce desire to own a pony shows no sign of waning, so it's a genre that will never run out of readers.

The books are pretty formulaic, but that is the fun of them (and of so many other series of books such as the Sleepover Club stories, the *Princess Diaries*, Biggles adventures and the Nancy Drew and Hardy Boys books in America). They are loved by their readers precisely because they know what they are going to get, and they offer the reader the wish-fulfilment they seek.

Picking just one pony book is difficult, but *Wish for a Pony* by Monica Edwards is an excellent representative, and has a title that sums up perfectly the dreams of its readers. It's all wonderfully exciting and dramatic, and a great reminder of just how many children (especially girls) really do wish for a pony and go through long pony-mad phases, all without any hope of ever having their wish granted.

IDEAS FOR PONY-MAD READERS

 Turn a bedroom into a pony shrine. In *Wish for a Pony* Tamzin is given the freedom to decorate her bedroom as she wishes, and plans to make it into a "horse-room" by collecting collect horsey pictures, horse bookends and horse brasses, and having horse curtains. She and her mother decorate the walls with prints of horses, and a huge paper frieze of horse drawings traced from photographs and calendars and outlined in black ink. For pony pictures, cut up calendars and magazines.

- Trace pictures of ponies with soft pencils and tracing paper.
- Do as Tamzin does and use chalks to draw ponies on a blackboard to improve life-drawing skills, or learn to draw them with pencils.
- Pretend to be a rider by setting up riding jumps in the garden, on a beach or in an open space. Use a stick for a crop, wear any hard hat, and leggings for jodhpurs.
- Learn to recognise the different breeds of pony from books, magazines and postcards. Ask your local stables whether you can help them or watch their ponies and horses being groomed and exercised.
- Go to a farm to see and touch ponies and horses, or book a few lessons or a ride.

Tell Fortunes

WHEN YOU ARE YOUNG THE FUTURE stretches out a long, long way ahead of you. There's so much that might happen, so many possibilities, so many options, that it's no wonder children love a little fortune-telling. It's good to have something to fill the void, even if it is patent nonsense ('You will have thirty children') or a downright impossibility ('You will marry a frog').

There will always be takers for fortune-telling, which is why children love turning the process into a performance. This is exactly what Richmal Crompton's William does when he stands in for Miss Drew ('Woman of Mystery') in 'The Fête – and Fortune'. William dons her special gown to mask his face and, by means of a pack of fortune-telling cards, he takes his revenge upon his teacher, brother and sister all of whom have treated him unfairly (so he believes, although he is blissfully unaware of the extent to which he has tested their patience):

"You've been hard on a boy jus' lately. He – he may not live very long. You've time to make up to him."

The outcome is better than even William could have predicted and he gets all he wants in the way of sweets, chocolates, trifle, pineapple and ice cream, as well as solicitous enquiries about his health. And in doing so, he demonstrates both the entertainment value and ridiculousness of fortune-telling.

✺ PRACTICAL ✺

There is a wealth of information about fortune-telling methods on the internet, but all young fortune-tellers really need to do is maintain the spirit of true fortune-telling and make it up as they go along.

➤ Cards: children's versions of tarot cards are available, but I think it's better to use an ordinary pack of cards to which new meanings and fortunes are ascribed, so that any suggestion of witchcraft is avoided and younger children are not made nervous.

➤ Crystal ball gazing: the most outlandish and pretend of all, as the 'ball' will probably be a glass paperweight, balloon, sports ball, crumpled ball of aluminium foil, or a ball covered with cling film. This type of fortune-telling makes a good parlour or party game. The fortune-teller can dress up in bright flowing clothes with a sash or scarf around the waist, jewellery, earrings and bandana, and apply plenty of daring make-up for effect. Tea cosies make very effective turbans. Customers can be received in a den or in a specially created 'tent'.

➤ Reading tea leaves or coffee grounds. The fortune-teller drains the liquid by swirling the tea then pouring it off carefully so that the tea leaves or coffee grounds make a shape/letter/symbol in the bottom of the cup. Although there are many accepted readings of these shapes and symbols, it's possible to make up new versions and apply them to give more extravagant and/or surprising fortunes.

➤ Palm-reading: the writing hand is 'read' by interpreting the hand-shape, lines, bumps, fingers and fingernails. Again, the standard meanings can be applied or new ones can be invented.

➤ Creating horoscopes: a newspaper or magazine will provide details of star signs and their dates, ideas and typical horoscope styles. The fortune-teller can draw up predictions for friends and family for the next day, the coming week or the year ahead.

HOW TO MAKE A PAPER FORTUNE-TELLER

Paper fortune-tellers are very easy to make – but it's also very easy to forget how to do so. So here are instructions for first-timers and those who haven't made one in a while. Thinking up the fortunes is the best part, but colouring and decorating them can be very enjoyable, too. Any size and colour of paper can be used (exercise books were the usual material at my school) but it's best to start with plain A4 paper.

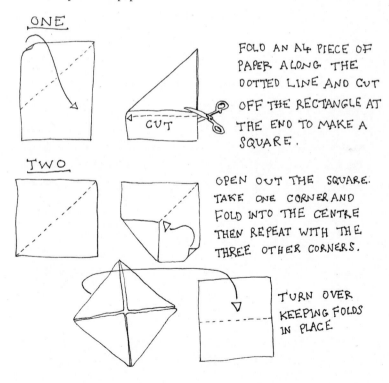

ONE

FOLD AN A4 PIECE OF PAPER ALONG THE DOTTED LINE AND CUT OFF THE RECTANGLE AT THE END TO MAKE A SQUARE.

CUT

TWO

OPEN OUT THE SQUARE. TAKE ONE CORNER AND FOLD INTO THE CENTRE THEN REPEAT WITH THE THREE OTHER CORNERS.

TURN OVER KEEPING FOLDS IN PLACE.

THREE

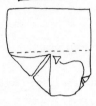 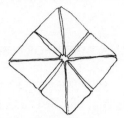 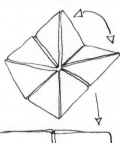

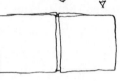

TAKE ONE CORNER AND FOLD INTO
THE CENTRE THEN REPEAT WITH
THE THREE OTHER CORNERS.
FOLD IN HALF WITH THE SQUARE
EDGES (NOT POINTS') ON THE OUTSIDE.

FOUR

USING BOTH HANDS,
PUSH YOUR THUMBS
AND FORE FINGERS
INTO THE OUTER
FLAPS TO OPEN UP
AND MOVE THE
FORTUNE- TELLER
BACKWARDS AND
FORWARDS, LEFT
AND RIGHT.

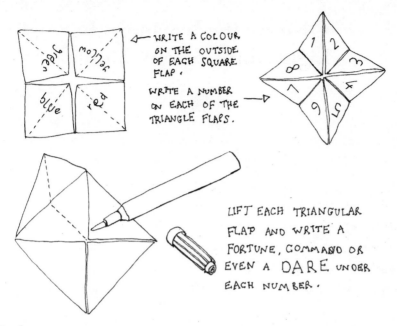

WRITE A COLOUR ON THE OUTSIDE OF EACH SQUARE FLAP.

WRITE A NUMBER ON EACH OF THE TRIANGLE FLAPS.

LIFT EACH TRIANGULAR FLAP AND WRITE A FORTUNE, COMMAND OR EVEN A DARE UNDER EACH NUMBER.

To play:

1. Refold the fortune-teller and put your forefingers and thumbs in the flaps to keep it closed.

2. Ask someone to choose a colour.

3. Spell out the colour, moving the fortune-teller backwards and forwards with each letter.

4. Ask the person to select a number from the inside. Move the fortune-teller in and out the right number of times.

5. Now ask the person to choose one of the numbers. Lift up the flap and read out their fortune.

NOTE: Adults should make sure a fortune-teller's power does not go to his/her head and that no one is upset or victimised.

Observe the World by the Light of the Silvery Moon

GOING OUTSIDE AT NIGHT TO LOOK at the world by the light of the silvery moon is guaranteed to give you shivers and tingles, and a sense of fairy-tale. It's a lovely Thing to Do in your pyjamas, and yet all too often we forget to take the time to observe the way in which familiar objects and scenes are transformed by moonlight.

The best moonlight stories and poems remind us, though. Take, for example, the enchanting description of Maria's arrival at her new home, the poetically named Moonacre, in *The Little White Horse* by Elizabeth Goudge, "... a place so beautiful that it seemed hardly to be of this world."

"It was all silver ... the trunks of tall trees rose from grass so silvered by the moonlight that it glimmered like water. The trees were not thickly planted, and beautiful glades opened between them, showing glimpses of an ebony sky set with silver stars. Nothing moved. It was all quite still, as though enchanted under the moon. The silvery tracery of twigs and branches above the silver tree trunks was so delicate that the moonlight sifted through it like a fine film of silver dust."

Then Maria sees a silver owl, a silver rabbit and a group of silver deer and "she thought she saw a little white horse". Thus the scene is set for this beautiful story.

The great thing about looking at the world by moonlight is that it's so incredibly easy to do, yet endlessly magical. All children love the goosebump sensation brought on by a mixture of fear, awe and excitement, and a bright, silvery moon never fails to produce this.

 **PRACTICAL**

➤ It's worth children investigating basic astronomy so that they know what to look for and can recognise crescent and gibbous moons, first and last quarters, waxing and waning, full and new moons. It's easy to find details of the current moon cycle by looking in a newspaper, and there is plenty of easy-to-understand and visual material, including moon cycles for months to come, on the internet.

➤ Googling 'phases moon' produces masses of useful lunar information and plenty of charts showing the eerily beautiful phases of the moon. In fact, the internet has the clearest, and most accessible, current information about the moon. There are also various children's books about the night sky and astronomy, but these are often too detailed and technical for what is needed here: a sense of wonder and a measure of poetry.

➤ A night-time walk in the countryside or on a beach is the best way to see the transformational effect the moon has on the earth. Children adore being out after dark, anyway, and there is nothing like watching them see their world in a new light for renewing your own vision.

➤ Hand-drawn moonlight pictures are always highly effective. Dark blue or black paper, and white and pale colour crayons, pencils, chalk or oil pastels, glitter and/or sequins, tinfoil and glue, give children plenty of scope to create moonlit scenes the morning after the night before.

Idle Pleasures

PARENTS AND CHILDREN ALL HAVE GREAT expectations. It's just that they are often not the same. Driven by a fear of wasting time, parents often think the timetable of childhood should be full of improving activities and useful skills. But if you ask the average child what they'd like to do when they have some free time, it almost certainly won't be more violin practice or a judo competition or extra maths. It may come as a shock, but quite often most children would be perfectly happy doing nothing – or what looks like nothing to grown-ups.

Because even when children are doing nothing they are doing something, and the best children's books support and explain the wisdom of allowing children to follow their natures and indulge in idle pleasures when it suits them.

And the wonderful thing about these apparently idle pleasures is that once you are free from pressure and schedules, it's possible to let one activity flow gently into another. In fact, idle pleasures are far from random and unstructured; they possess an inner logic of their own, one that often defies adults. Just look at how the activities of characters in books by E. Nesbit, Astrid Lindgren, Philippa Pearce and Anthony Buckeridge flow, with one thing feeding and inspiring another. Everything is connected and linked, but unhurried and unpressurised, absorbing and delightful. So children who have inner resources from reading books will never be bored and at a loose end. As this chapter shows, there are plenty of literary equivalents to navel-gazing and bubble-blowing (both perfectly respectable occupations, I think) to keep children happily absorbed and occupied in idle moments, but with absolutely no great expectations at all.

Doing Nothing in the Garden

CHILDREN ARE SO LUCKY. They can spend an entire sunny summer's afternoon lying on their tummies on the grass watching the fascinating miniature universe of bugs and insects while the rest of the big, wide world rushes by.

The best literary exponent of the art of doing apparently nothing yet learning a huge amount is Gerald Durrell in *My Family and Other Animals*. It helps that his interest in the natural world is awakened when he moves to the enchanted island of Corfu, which is host to a vast number of species. He begins his education in the garden, which he comes to realise with delight is a "multi-coloured Lilliput" and, indeed he learns far more here than he ever does in the formal lessons he detests.

He finds all kinds of wonderment: tiny spiders whose body colours change to match their host flower, furry blue carpenter bees, sleek and neat hawkmoths, astonishing lacewing flies and a vast range of lady-birds in all sorts of spotty colour combinations:

"...on the rose-stems... lady-birds moved like newly painted toys; lady-birds pale red with large black spots; lady-birds apple-red with brown spots; lady-birds orange with grey-and-black freckles."

Once Gerald has mastered the art of looking and seeing, he sets off to explore the world beyond the garden, his early lessons in garden naturalism having taught him the value of truly looking and learning.

 **PRACTICAL**

The natural world is a gift to any observant child. Even the smallest garden or corner of a field or park (or any outdoor place for that matter) is home to a diversity of little insect worlds that can be explored. It doesn't have to be anything exotic, either, in order to fascinate. Common-or-garden creatures such as lady-birds, ants, beetles (especially magnificent stag beetles which appear in all sorts of suburban spots in summer) bees, millipedes, earwigs, lacewings, shield bugs and spiders can afford hours of entertainment.

The best way to encourage budding naturalists is to read them books such as *My Family and Other Animals*, point out the teeming life that lurks all around us, provide supplies of jam jars, small boxes, nets and simple guides for identification. Then stand back and let them get on with it.

149

Chalking It Up

SOMETIMES IT'S THE SIMPLE, tried and tested things that are the best. Take chalks, for example. Chalks may seem like something out of the dark ages these days, but I urge you to reconsider their merits. Just think of all that can be done with a cheap box of chalks. People can be taught how to read, write and do sums on blackboards. Children can enjoy endless games of hopscotch on outdoor surfaces. They can play noughts and crosses all day long. They can create spectacular wall graffiti. They can attempt to chalk artistic portraits to earn a bob or two. And they can emulate Bert the Match Man in P.L. Travers' *Mary Poppins* and make wonderfully realistic pavement pictures, pictures that are worthy of being hung in the Royal Academy, according to Mary Poppins.

A piece of pavement or path or playground or wall, and a few chalks, are all children need to create a window on a different world. Drawing and colouring and playing with chalks is oh so simple, but completely absorbing, creative and as interactive as you like. In fact, I'd bet that quite a few adults would still be more than happy to pick up a few chalks themselves, get their hands dusty and hop, skip and jump back into old times.

PRACTICAL

- Chalks are amazingly versatile and have all sorts of uses, especially when something washable, non-permanent and non-toxic is needed.
- Chalk is essential for hopscotch.
- And for making pavement pictures.

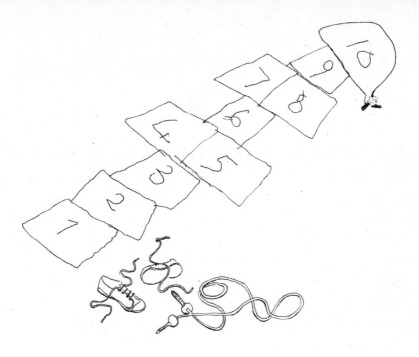

- And for chalking lines for tightropes, goal areas, tennis courts, volleyball courts, territories and magic circles.
- Chalks are worth taking or buying on holiday because they can be put to so many uses. For example, pebbles can be dotted with chalk and used to play dominoes on the beach.
- And dolls can be spotted with chalk to make them ill with measles or chickenpox.
- When the chalk pictures or graffiti or grids are no longer needed, they can be washed off with warm water and a scrubbing brush. The cleaning-up process can be a great excuse for a water fight.
- Finally, children still love blackboards even though they are almost obsolete in schools. Together with a box of chalks, a blackboard can enable all sorts of entertaining role-playing games.

Have Fun with Tongue-Twisters

WHEN THE INIMITABLE JENNINGS and Darbishire decide to create their very own fictional detective in Anthony Buckeridge's *Jennings Goes to School* they unwittingly invent one of the best tongue-twisters I've come across.

Before they start lisping and slurring and twisting their tongues, however, they make the brilliant and observant discovery that "unless your name consisted of a single syllable and … a two-syllabled first name, you could never hope to succeed in the world of crime detection. Sherlock Holmes, Sexton Blake, Nelson Lee, Dixon Hawke, Falcon Swift, Ferrers Locke – all the best detectives were most careful to have the correct number of syllables to their names."

They decide to follow suit and call their detective 'Flixton Slick – Super Sleuth'. But they soon find out that not only have they come up with a name worthy of a 1930s film noir character, they have also created a nightmare of articulation.

"Darbishire rolled the syllables round his tongue… 'It's a bit tricky to say…you keep getting "sloops" in it if you say it too fast.'"

Try it and see.

PRACTICAL

Tongue-twisters are great levellers (no doubt many an eminent person would have difficulty saying 'Peggy Babcock' fast and furiously) and this is why children love them.

➤ Tongue-twisters are a good way of passing car journeys or long, wet school playtimes, so it's worth having a few ready to try. For a good supply beyond the usual 'She sells sea shells', 'Peter Piper' and 'Red lorry, yellow lorry', search the internet for them and you'll find all sorts of verbal torture such as this, the most difficult tongue-twister in the English language according to *Guinness World Records*: 'The sixth sick sheikh's sixth sheep's sick.'

➤ Of course, it's also possible for children to do what Jennings and Darbishire do, and make up new and original tongue-twisters (and detectives).

Be a Scarecrow for a Day

ALTHOUGH THE ORIGINAL FICTIONAL Worzel Gummidge is preferable to the screen Worzel Gummidge, it's all too easy to see why he became a TV superstar. He's a walking, talking, rude, sulky, badly behaved, badly dressed scarecrow who isn't frightened of breaking social rules. He's also dirty – he's a scarecrow, for goodness' sake – and children love a bit of muck. So it's not surprising that when Susan and John in Barbara Euphan Todd's *Worzel Gummidge Again* realise there's an opportunity to dress up as a scarecrow, they jump at the chance.

There's to be a garden fête in a nearby village, and the children are initially reluctant to go:

"Fêtes generally mean best uncomfortable clothes – nails sore from sharp cleaning, heads aching after the hair-brush and faces smelling of soaped flannel."

But then they are told there will be a fancy-dress competition and, rejecting suggestions to go as Miss Muffet and Little Tommy Tucker ("that sounded a perfectly horrid idea"), they decide to go as scarecrows and enjoy this thrilling and unusual experience: "It felt queer and very exciting to be allowed to go to a garden fête with dirty hands and faces, and with hair that had been ruffled up on purpose."

Needless to say, they don't win the prize for the prettiest fancy dress, but they do win the prize that carries far greater kudos: the one for the most original costume.

PENNY FOR THE GUY

◈ **PRACTICAL** ◈

The great thing about dressing up as a scarecrow is that a child can be as revolting as they like. Walnut leaves and blackberry juice smeared across their face, bits of sacking and straw for clothing, muddy boots, old coats and a good whiff of the countryside are just what's needed. Here's how John and Susan do it.

HOW TO DRESS UP AS A BOY SCARECROW

"John rubbed his face all over with crushed walnut leaves until it was a streaky brown. He turned his oldest pair of flannel trousers inside out, and put a broomstick handle through the sleeves of Gummidge's coat… luckily the coat was much too big, so he knew that even after he had padded himself out with hay he would be able to keep his own arms out of sight and hanging down quite comfortably. There was a very old bowler hat in the barn, and this was quite a good fit after it had been padded out with hay."

HOW TO DRESS UP AS A GIRL SCARECROW

"Susan used walnut leaves and blackberry juice for her face. She tied a bit of sacking round her waist for a skirt, turned another bit of sacking into a cloak, borrowed a check apron… stuffed some brown woollen gloves with paper and twisted a fish bass into something that didn't quite look like either a hat or a sun-bonnet."

More suggestions for the scarecrow look: old belts, scarves, jeans, dungarees, overalls, jackets, shirts, straw hats, wellies, old boots, rubber gloves, mittens, string to hold the outfit together. Add tufts of straw to complete the effect.

MAKE A SCARECROW

Alternatively, you could make a scarecrow. The possibilities are endless, from a very basic scarecrow to one with personality and an interesting/dubious taste in clothes. One year, we made a tall lady scarecrow with a crinoline skirt – a wigwam of short canes that came up to her 'waist' – and grew nasturtiums up the canes to create a floral frock effect. She wore some of my old clothes on her top half and her bottom half was eventually surrounded by annuals, and ended up looking quite grand and lady-of-the-manorish.

■→ Use two strong stakes (or wooden broom handles) to make the basic upright and horizontal arms structure and tie firmly with garden twine. Push the main stake into the ground and position 10–12 bamboo canes in a circle (approximately 45 to 50 cm radius). Bring the tops of the canes together at the stake to form a wigwam (you'll need two people to do this) and tie securely with twine. Plant two or three nasturtium seeds or a couple of nasturtium seedlings at the base of each cane (see page 130 for more on growing nasturtiums). Another idea would be to grow French climbing beans or runner beans up the scarecrow's skirt and on up her body and arms. Add a head to the top of the stake; use a clay plant pot with a face drawn on, or a pair of tights – stuff the end of one of the legs with straw or old clothes, tie with string and cut. Add clothes and accessories (hats, gloves, scarves) to suit your scarecrow lady.

■→ For more scarecrow inspiration and instructions, visit a scarecrow festival. There are a growing number of these and their dedicated websites are an excellent source of ideas and amusement. Recommendations in the United Kingdom: Abbotsley (Cambridgeshire), Kettlewell (Yorkshire) and Hayling Island (Hampshire) for high quality and whackiness.

Stand On Your Hands

ISN'T IT LOVELY WHEN THINGS TURN out well after a summer of change? Or when things turn out well at any time? But what's the best way of celebrating a happy ending? Garnet in Elizabeth Enright's *Thimble Summer* has the answer:

"It was a good thing that Eric had taught her to do hand-stands and flip-ups, Garnet decided. It was very handy to know how to do one or two when you felt happy. Better than jumping. Better than yelling." And then she does a whole series of "handsprings" down the pasture to express her elation at the way her thimble summer has turned out.

Handstands, handsprings, cartwheels, somersaults, back flips and forward flips, and many other carefree frolics are some of the purest expressions of exuberance, playfulness and zest for life. If they can't walk on their hands on the beach like Kate in Eve Garnett's *The Family from One End Street*, skip in the garden like Mary in Frances Hodgson Burnett's *The Secret Garden*, spend ages upside down doing handstands against a wall with their dress tucked in their knickers like Magdalen Nabb's Josie Smith at the seaside, and run and leap and twirl and throw themselves about when they are young, when can they?

MORE CAREFREE FROLICS

The most convincing and endearing characters in children's books are often not the best behaved ones – usually because they are too busy living spontaneously and to the full instead of conforming to the expectations of parents and adults.

Eleanor H. Porter's Pollyanna sets a fine example to children of how to enjoy yourself and make the most of being young. When she arrives to live with her Aunt Polly she negotiates a period in her strict timetable of reading, music, sewing, cooking and tidying "just to live", so that she can wander, watch, play, climb, explore and be herself.

Everyone needs 'just living' time in their lives, especially children, and so here are a few more carefree frolics:

- Many children enjoy the exhilaration and tumbles that come with learning to ride a bike. Milly-Molly-Mandy, Billy Blunt and little-friend-Susan rattle and wobble and fall in buttercups, and have enormous fun on old cycles. Other, more seasoned, cyclists like Enid Blyton's Famous Five and Five Find-Outers pedal off on picnics and days out, whooshing down hills and enjoying the thrill of speed.

- The boys in Jennings' dormitory in Anthony Buckeridge's *Jennings Goes to School* use the beds as an airfield and leap over them to 'take off'.

- The Winnie-the-Pooh books by A.A. Milne contain a whole host of characters who are skilled in the art of 'just living' and have inspired many children to bounce like Tigger, jump like Roo, and sing songs like Pooh – his "Outdoor Song for Snowy Weather" is a classic ("The more it/SNOWS – tiddley pom…").

- My Naughty Little Sister in the book by Dorothy Edwards also has a talent for 'just living'. In the story with the 'good polite child', she gets out her toys, makes mud pies, eats gooseberries, races round the lawn, climbs the apple tree, shouts over the front gate to schoolchildren, and eats four cakes, three jam tarts and eight ginger biscuits, while the good, polite child barely moves speaks or eats for fear of getting dirty or behaving badly.

Have a Ride in a Wheelbarrow

WHEN OUR CHILDREN WERE LITTLE, there were many times when Simon and I were gardening and we would turn round to find a little, smiling, expectant child sitting in the wheelbarrow, hoping to be taken for a bumpy, hair-raising, white-knuckle ride round the garden. It was this illustration from Philippa Pearce's *Tom's Midnight Garden*, of the moment when a ghostly Tom hitches a ride in a wheelbarrow, that prompted memories of how much fun this form of garden or allotment transport can be. It's simple, it's easy and it's free. Alton Towers, Thorpe Park and all other theme parks, eat your hearts out — nothing beats a wheelbarrow ride for cheap thrills.

PRACTICAL

- If there is one thing that's needed for a good wheelbarrow ride, it has to be strong arms (like the gardener in the picture on the next page) so it's a great garden activity to organise when you have teenagers and older siblings and cousins around.
- Any wheelbarrow will do as long as the wheel goes round.
- Put a piece of sacking or an old blanket in the wheelbarrow to prevent children getting too filthy if it has been used recently for mucky jobs. This will also stop them sliding around too much and add a little padding when they are jolted about.
- Tipping out is a good way to end a ride. Piles of raked leaves or mown grass make soft landings.

🐞 Alternatively, hold old-fashioned body-wheelbarrow races in which one person is the wheelbarrow — hands on the ground, feet supported by the wheelbarrow pusher.

🐞 Or let children take toys and pets for wheelbarrow rides. Phoebe used to take our hens for rides in a wheelbarrow, which looked very eccentric but enjoyable.

🐞 Child-size mini-wheelbarrows are fantastic garden toys and can be put to a multitude of uses by imaginative children.

Beachcombing

WE ONCE SPENT A WHOLE WEEK'S holiday in Aldeburgh, Suffolk, reading in hammocks. One of the children's books we read was *Up the Steps*, a tale of smugglers and shipwrecks set in Aldeburgh and written by a local author, Nora Acheson. What struck us most was the fact that the characters in the book went looking for cornelian and amber on the very beach outside our holiday home.

So off we all went in search of treasure – but with no luck. In the end we resorted to buying a couple of small packets of unpolished amber in a local shop, and even considered scattering a packet over a section of beach so that we could return the next year, look for our amber, and triumphantly exclaim to everyone on the beach that we'd found some.

Nevertheless, we came to the conclusion that beachcombing is a great activity. It can be done at any time of the year and in any weather; in fact, the best finds are usually made after a spell of stormy weather when the sea has deposited all sorts of flotsam and jetsam on the beach and started to recede, revealing treasures such as shells, marine life, bits of rope, sea glass, ammonite fossils, amber, jet and exciting stones (heart-shaped, with a hole in the middle, a certain colour, stripy). Beachcombing is also one of the few activities that can be done by the entire family from the youngest, who get excited about seaweed, to the oldest, who are happy with the gentle pace.

 **PRACTICAL**

➤ Simply find a good beach and visit it when the tide is going out. Take a bag or wear clothes with pockets. And allow a little time to get your eye in, as they say in cricket, so that you focus clearly and can spot interesting objects and good finds.

➤ One of the great advantages of living on an island is that there is no shortage of great beaches for beachcombing. The following, though, are considered some of the best:

* Camber, East Sussex
* Newgate Beach, Pembrokshire
* Frinton Beach, Frinton-on-Sea, Essex
* Herne Bay East, Kent
* Barmston, East Yorkshire
* Combe Martin Beach, Devon
* Cresswell Dunes and Foreshore, Northumberland
* Runswick Bay, North Yorkshire
* Westward Ho! Devon
* Cowes, Isle of Wight

➤ Don't discount river banks for beachcombing. Garnet finds the solid silver thimble that she believes brings luck and good fortune on the sandy flats of the local river in *Thimble Summer* by Elizabeth Enright.

➤ Take a book about the seashore with you so you know what you are looking at.

Lazy Weekends

SO WE'VE SPENT A FEW HOURS OR perhaps a blissful summer's day indulging in idle pleasures, but what do we do with a whole weekend?

Once a child has started school, weekends take on a whole new complexion and become something to look forward to, something comforting and liberating at the end of a hard-working week. At last, after five days' effort, it's a time for yourself, and to be yourself.

Some families may find the idea of a comparatively empty and unstructured weekend crushing, but the writers of classic children's books would not agree. Just think of all their wonderfully resourceful characters: Enid Blyton's Secret Seven, Katy and her siblings in *What Katy Did*, Richmal Crompton's Outlaws and even Paddington Bear, all of whom view a lazy weekend as a welcome opportunity to be in control of their activities rather than being told what to do. These self-reliant, motivated characters (and a bear) are marvellous examples of the benefits of giving young people plenty of space at the weekend, and enough time to potter, to dabble, to dream, to imagine, to experiment, and to draw breath away from adults.

The children in books have what some modern readers might consider tedious and dull weekends. The past is a world without theme parks, leisure centres or swimming/skiing/tennis lessons (characters can only *wish* for riding lessons) and it's much more likely that letter-writing, Sunday school and church are on the agenda. But the difference between them and children today is that, apart from these obligations, the children are mostly free and let off the hook by adults. So what do they do? Do they hang around adults complaining that they're bored? They do not. They skedaddle before they are roped into chores, and do all the things children should do when they have the joy of two whole days off school. They disappear from sight, making the most of being around the house, scurrying off to create and use little hideaways, dens and retreats. They are only momentarily dismayed by wet weekends before organising and amusing themselves, keeping busy with clubs or making collections, being sociable, or even enjoying being alone.

For many, the ultimate lazy weekend activity is reading a book. How often, when a child says 'I'm bored', do we say 'Read a book'? Well, it's the right advice; by reading a book their boredom will be banished – once by the reading itself and again in the things they will be inspired to do. Or they can simply read this chapter.

Amuse Yourself on a Wet Afternoon

I AM A GREAT FAN OF BOREDOM. I think children should be left to get bored at home quite often, actually. Because it's only then that they begin to use their imagination and the resources available to amuse themselves. If they are never bored, they are never going to be able to solve the problem of boredom creatively and, goodness knows, sooner or later they will need that skill – especially in the long school holidays.

So it's ironic that I found some of the most ripping things to do on a wet afternoon in a book set in a school. Anthony Buckeridge's *Jennings Follows a Clue* opens with a wonderful scene of organised chaos: a room full of young boys who are keeping themselves busy on a wet Wednesday half-holiday. The setting is a typical, Spartan, Fifties boy's prep school. No frills, no comforts, no TV, no electronic hand-held games, no adults to organise every moment of the day. So the boys' imaginations flourish and they make the most of everything they have.

Odd pieces of wood become model yachts, biscuit tins are beaten into aeroplane wings, and a tea tray, stick, empty box and riding crop provide sound effects for a puppet theatre. Members of the wireless club listen to the radio on home-made sets while sportier boys play an improvised game of hockey with cricket stumps for sticks and a boxing glove for a ball. In the midst of all this mayhem and noise sit Jennings and Darbishire, fingers firmly in ears, playing chess.

And the phrase 'I'm bored!' is never uttered. Not that anyone would hear it or heed it above the happy, purposeful, creative din.

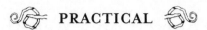 PRACTICAL

➤ Model aeroplanes and boats:

Shop-bought model kits are fantastic for some children, but can be intensely frustrating for others. It can be far more rewarding to spend an afternoon creating a one-off, unique model aeroplane or boat or ship using what's available in the home: hammers, bits of wood, biscuit tins and plenty of creative licence. If you don't have biscuit tins or wood, cardboard, paper, glue, paper clips, rubber bands will do the job. Balsa wood is still a brilliant model material, though, and can be bought from craft and hobby suppliers.

➤ Indoor ball games:

Amazingly, these don't automatically wreck the house and break windows if you supply small, soft balls (eg mini-footballs and rugby balls or beanbags). Left to their own devices, children often create wonderful, complex indoor games, leagues and tournaments.

➤ Puppet theatre:

Incredibly easy. Children are often happy just to kneel behind a chair and settee and make their puppets perform along the back. 'Puppets' can be as simple as soft toys or Barbie dolls, different-coloured socks on hands (maybe with wool, felt bits and bobbles glued on) or simply hands with features drawn on with felt-tip pens. It's also possible to make a very simple puppet theatre with a large cardboard box (electrical appliance shops are a good source): spray-paint, paint or decorate the box, cut out a rectangle for the stage area, create scenery and backdrops, add curtains if desired.

Glove puppets can be made by gluing wool, googly eyes (from craft shops) and pieces of felt on to the fingers of the gloves to create separate characters. Or simple figures cut out of magazines or drawn on card can be glued to lolly sticks.

Write or improvise a script and create sound effects.

→ Make a transistor radio:

Building a transistor radio is something that is sadly out of fashion now, despite the fact that it is possible to make one relatively easily at home and even out of domestic materials. Good, detailed, technical instructions can be found on the internet (google 'build home wireless radio') or consult that classic title *Making a Transistor Radio* (Ladybird Books, 1972, reprinted 2008 in the *Vintage Ladybird Box for Boys*). An adult's help may be needed, but it would be an excellent project for a wet afternoon.

Enjoy a Weekend Retreat

WEEKEND RETREATS SHOULD NOT BE just the province of stressed-out adults – children need their space, too. And if they are allowed to retreat, well then, the adults get more space, too. Children don't need to disappear too far away for their weekend retreats, but can be safe and happy close by in places like attics, lofts, sheds and barns.

In *What Katy Did* by Susan Coolidge Katy, her siblings and her best friend Cecy Hall often retreat en masse to various favourite, private places and their Aunt Izzy can't understand their "queer notions about getting off into holes and corners and poke-away places". On rainy Saturday afternoons they head off to the loft to enjoy a "splendiferous" feast with stories, verses, performances and the ceremonial passing round of a bottle of vinegar and water. They eat delicious-sounding caraway cookies with scalloped edges and suck sticks of cinnamon; it makes something very ordinary – a group of children in a loft – appear quite marvellous and provides a charming idea to copy.

Katy et al are not the only ones who escape from family life to a private space. Books contain lots of children who are happily ensconced and perched up high in lofts and attics, surrounded by the discarded and stored jumble and treasures of the house.

Pollyanna's retreat is her attic bedroom, Jo in Louisa May Alcott's *Little Women* loves nothing more than reading and writing and eating apples in her garret room, and the Railway Children hold their 'councils' in the loft. Sara Crewe's attic bedroom in *A Little Princess* by Frances Hodgson Burnett is at first a bare and lonely place, but in time it becomes a place of refuge, comfort, companionship and hot tea and muffins. Another weekend retreat is the ham and pepper and onion-filled, spicy-smelling attic in Laura Ingall Wilder's *The Little House in the Big Woods* where Laura and Mary go to play in winter: "Often the wind howled outside with a cold and lonesome sound. But in the attic Laura and Mary played house with the squashes and pumpkins and everything was snug and cosy." And Jo Ruggles in *The Family from One End Street* by Eve Garnett reminds us of one of the best weekend retreats of all: the cinema, where you can, like him, indulge in hours of fantasy and escapism on a Saturday afternoon.

IDEAS FOR A WEEKEND RETREAT

A loft, attic or garret is not essential. Retreats can be taken in spare rooms, in indoor and outdoor dens, in tents and any 'hole', 'corner' or 'poke-away place'. The following are suggestions for what to do:

- Form a club
- Tell stories
- Write a play
- Dress up and put on a show
- Practice magic tricks
- Tell fortunes
- Learn new codes
- Set up a detective agency
- Write a newspaper
- Eat home-made biscuits (see page 171)
- Go to see a film. Many cinemas still have children's weekend matinees with vastly reduced ticket prices, so it's worth checking with your local cinema(s) in advance.

Make an Indoor Den

TO THE ADULT, IT MAY LOOK LIKE a pile of pillows/a mess of blankets/a jumble sale or as though a bomb has gone off / burglars have been in/a stranger has set up camp in your living room. But to the child it's a wonderful den, a bandits' hideaway, a smugglers' cave, a shipwrecked boat, a desert or treasure island, a hospital, a shop, a prison, a post office, an igloo, a meeting room, a reading room, a place to play cards or board-games. Or maybe it's a robbers' cave inspired by John Masefield's *The Box of Delights*?

"Robber Tea was one of Kay's delights. It was a game played only in winter evenings, in the dark old study that had shelves full of old books, and old guns on the walls above the shelves."

Kay and his friends begin by drawing the curtains to make the room dark. Then they build up the fire, drag the table to one side of the room against the bookshelves, and cover the table and the adjoining chairs with heavy curtains to make an 'inner cave'. This they light with lanterns that have coloured glass slides to create a suitably exciting atmosphere, and finally they toast sausages and bread on the fire before retiring to their robbers' cave to eat them.

All children have an innate desire to create dens and hideaways, and little private places where adults are not allowed and where they can indulge in fantasies and act out new and different roles. And because of this I've always been very indulgent towards den-making in my family; as long as the adults have somewhere to sit when the children have gone to bed (I draw the line at *all* the settee cushions being removed), a den can stay where it is for the duration of the game.

Making a den is an ideal winter and weekend thing to do; the cold and dark make everyone want to cosy up in a snug little cave and a weekend offers the perfect amount of time to develop and exploit the den. Relax – it won't be there for ever.

PRACTICAL

- Provide a room or spot where the den can stay if it looks as though the game is going to last a while – there is nothing worse for a child/children than to have to dismantle a beloved den while the game is in full flow because others need the space.
- Allow the game to last as long as necessary but insist that the robbers help tidy up afterwards.

SUGGESTIONS FOR DEN-MAKERS (AND INHABITANTS)

- Dens under tables are quick and easy to make, or you may need to push bits of furniture together to make private spaces that can be covered with sheets and blankets.
- Furnish with duvets, cushions and pillows.
- Light the den with torches or battery-powered safety lamps.
- Arrange for delivery of special foods on a trays (see page 286).
- Make sure books, games and packs of cards are available if you need them.
- Cultivate the grown-up art of pretending the den isn't there and that you can't see anyone or anything.

Go Puddle-Jumping in Wellies

"**IF IT HAD BEEN RAINING ALFIE LIKED** to go stamping about in mud and walking through puddles, splish, splash, SPLOSH!"

For more than a quarter of a century children have been inspired by *Alfie's Feet* to go puddle-jumping and mud-splashing in their wellies. This is not to say that Shirley Hughes invented these simple activities; it's just that she was the first to make them look so enticing in her enduring and endearing story. With her inimitable style, she manages to capture one of the timeless joys and pleasures of childhood and turns it into an 'I want to do that!' activity.

Such are her powers of suggestion, I'm willing to bet there are also quite a few adults who echo this sentiment when they read *Alfie's Feet*. And why not? Puddle-jumping and mud-splashing keep us young at heart, even if we can't all stay for ever young like Alfie.

PRACTICAL

➤ Wellies are enjoying a phase of renewed popularity which means it's no longer a case of 'any colour as long as it's black'. There are all sorts of colourful and patterned wellies to get children and adults puddle-jumping and mud-splashing. Heck, there are even 'festival wellies' for truly cool muddy events. Look at The Welly Shop (www.thewellyshop.com).

➤ The beauty of puddle-jumping and mud-splashing is that they can be done anywhere and are great urban and rural activities for little children

who need to get out of the house regularly.

➤ Having said that, there is nothing to stop older children enjoying a spot of puddle-jumping. A friend's family has a New Year's Day tradition: they go on a long walk and the three children (now teenagers) and their friends have a competition to see who can get the wettest while jumping in puddles. Their wellies are emptied into measuring jugs when they get home, and a prize is awarded. Warm drinks and Christmas cake follow.

➤ Another charming perennial wellie-wearer is Josie Smith in the books by Magdalen Nabb. Highly recommended for young readers and for reading together.

Club Together

ALTHOUGH WE MAY FIND OURSELVES in the Groucho Marx mould when we get older (he said he didn't want to belong to any club that would accept him as a member), the majority of children are naturally clubbable. They want to be accepted, to be part of the group, the crowd, the gang, which is why they love the idea of creating clubs that add a little glamour, purpose, structure and importance to shared interests, no matter how trivial, and stamp them with a badge of exclusivity.

No wonder books that feature clubs have been thriving for years and continue to do so. Just think of favourite clubby books, and fond memories of exciting reads and wishful thinking will come flooding back.

First there is the secret society, the club inspired by wartime undercover espionage. This category is led by the Secret Seven and the Five Find-Outer books by Enid Blyton which set the bar very high when it comes to club rules with meetings in proper meeting places, decent catering, badges, passwords and results. And there should be an honourable mention of the club in Malcolm Saville's *Lone Pine* books, a secret society operating in wartime England.

Next there's the group or gang of friends who live apparently dull lives but want to have adventures and make life more exciting. Top of the list here are the inimitable Outlaws, the juvenile anarchists created by Richmal Crompton and led by William Brown. But also worth reading about is the Gang of the Black Hand in Eve Garnett's *The Family from One End Street* which meets in a disused kiln every Saturday afternoon to share the adventures each member is supposed to have had during the week (the one who tells the most thrilling is elected 'Chief Gangster' for a week).

Or there's the group of children who create clubs to entertain and amuse, and to make the most of being together. The four March girls in *Little Women* by Louisa May Alcott set up the Dickens-inspired, rather earnest Pickwick Club with literary aliases, badges, a newspaper, formal meetings and the Busy Bee Society dedicated to useful pursuits such as knitting, reading, sketching and sewing in the summer vacation. All very worthy but really very sophisticated and rather inspirational.

And then there's the club in which the members literally club together to make the most of their resources. The Saturday Club (or I.S.A.A.C., The Independent Saturday Afternoon Adventure Club) formed by the Melendy children in *The Saturdays*, part of the well-loved Melendy Quartet by Elizabeth Enright, is a wonderful example of sharing for the common good; they can't all do what they want every weekend, so they pool their money and take it in turns to have a Manhattan adventure.

PRACTICAL

The best place to start when it comes to clubs is the books themselves (they are full of excellent ideas) but here are a few practical suggestions:

- Purpose: the children will have to decide this (but bear in mind it might be 'secret') and, ultimately, any purpose will serve. It could even be the Tropical Fish Collectors Club (one of the clubs the Melendy children formed before I.S.A.A.C).

- Club name: acronyms work well, although 'S.S.' for the Secret Seven may be too politically incorrect for some. Expect many fallings-out before agreement is reached.

- Badges/passwords/aliases/ID cards/hand-stamps: all optional but great fun.

- Meeting place: once a club has been formed, a meeting place is needed. It could be a summer house or shed (this is what Enid Blyton's characters tend to use), a bedroom, a playhouse, an attic or loft, or a space under the stairs/in the bushes/up a tree.

- Meetings: private but food and drink provided by parents will be more than welcome (Janet's and Peter's mother in the Secret Seven books is happy to let them have enough lemonade and buns for six children and a dog every time there is a meeting in her garden).

- Pet: optional, but dogs are very useful for detective clubs (see Secret Seven, Five Find-Outers).

- Activities: espionage and detective work, 'Busy Bee' pastimes), sharing stories while eating toffee, putting on a show, writing a newspaper, inventing and using codes.

Form a Saturday Afternoon Adventure Club (and visit an art gallery)

THE SATURDAYS BY ELIZABETH ENRIGHT features the four Melendy children when they are living in Manhattan. It is the charming story of how they pool their pocket money and form a Saturday Afternoon Adventure Club so that they can each take it in turns to do what they want on a Saturday.

When it's ten-year-old Randy's turn to set foot on the streets of Manhattan alone, she finds that "the sense of independence is intoxicating". She enjoys a spot of window-shopping (Tiffany's, Woolworth's) before paying 75 cents to go into a gallery on 57th Street where "pretty soon she forgot about everything but the pictures". She has a good time looking at the paintings at her own pace when "all of a sudden she came to the picture that was hers, her very own one" and she takes possession of it, so to speak, by imprinting it on her memory.

"It was very easy to make this picture alive. Randy stared at it fixedly, hardly breathing, hardly thinking, and pretty soon she thought she could smell the mixture of damp and earth and burning leaves and smoke from distant chimney pots ..."

And then, when she has just about made it her own, she bumps into old Mrs Oliphant, who astounds her by saying she was the model for the girl in the painting, then whisks her off to a posh hotel for a refined tea with dainty yellow and pink petits fours "in a large room full of little tables, gilt chairs, mirrors and palms in fancy pots" and even a three-piece orchestra...

It's a wonderful big-city afternoon adventure, but at the heart of Randy's day out is the even greater adventure of discovering the power of paintings to move and engage the imagination, to tell stories, to evoke atmosphere and to transport the viewer. And this is the sort adventure that can last a lifetime.

PRACTICAL

- A visit to an art gallery with tea afterwards is a lovely thing to do with children from a very early age (I would say from about six or seven). The trick is not to stay too long or try to do too much.
- Then go to a café or tea shop or posh hotel and enjoy a little treat.
- Favourite galleries in London to visit with children are Tate Modern, Tate Britain, the National Gallery, the National Portrait Gallery and the Imperial War Museum. Many have activities at the weekends and in holidays – look at the relevant website for details. Tate Britain has a fantastic art trolley at weekends.
- Smaller collections can be less daunting for children. Sheffield, Reading, Bristol, Lincoln, Bournemouth, Norwich and Cambridge art galleries are all recommended as are the galleries (and café) at Salt's Mill near Bradford (www.saltsmill.org.uk)
- Don't forget there is also plenty of art outdoors; sculpture parks are perfect for children and they can run around missing out what they don't like and concentrating on the pieces that do appeal. recommend the Cass Sculpture Foundation in Hampshire (www.sculpture.org), the Barbara Hepworth museum and sculpture garden in St Ives (www.tate.org/stives/hepworth), the Yorkshire Sculpture Park www.ysp.co.uk, the Hannah Peschar Sculpture Garden www.hannahpescharsculpture.com and the sculpture trail in Grizedale Forest in the Lake District.

10 books to read under a blanket in autumn

1. *Autumn Term*, Antonia Forest (hearty hiking)

2. ***Josie Smith in Autumn,* Magdalen Nabb (blackberrying and Bonfire Night)**

3. *Anne of Green Gables*, L.M. Montgomery (the glory of nature)

4. *Daddy-Long-Legs*, Jean Webster (starting college)

5. ***Danny the Champion of World,* Roald Dahl (pheasant-shooting season)**

6. The *Mystery of the Spiteful Letters*, Enid Blyton (day trips to Burnham Beeches)

7. *The Adventures of Milly-Molly-Mandy*, Joyce Lankester Brisley (heart-warming stories)

8. ***Worzel Gummidge Again,* Barbara Euphan Todd (autumn on a farm)**

9. *Jennings Goes to School*, Anthony Buckeridge (first term at new school)

10. *Five Go on a Hike Together*, Enid Blyton (knapsacks and barley sugar)

Red Letter Days

CHILDREN IN BOOKS ENJOY SOME truly lovely red letter days. There are marvellous birthday celebrations like Petrova's birthday picnic in *Ballet Shoes*, big days out to the seaside for Josie Smith and Paddington Bear, and the Ruggles in *The Family from One End Street*. There are exciting excursions to castles in books by Enid Blyton, and adventures in a maze in *The Enchanted Castle*, and there are days that start out quite ordinary but end up being red letter days, like the day of the paperchase in *The Railway Children*.

To read about a red letter day in a book is to learn that much of the pleasure is in the planning, the anticipation, the mental crossing off of dates until the big day itself arrives, the living through the ordinary days printed in black while hugging to yourself the knowledge that there's a bright red one ahead — like the Ruggles family who relish every little detail in advance and spread the enjoyment of a single day over several weeks. Children also learn that sometimes you never know when a red letter day is going to happen spontaneously, when everything — people, place, weather, atmosphere, birthday cake — conspires to make an event, like a birthday picnic, one to look back on with happy memories.

But maybe a single red letter day is not sufficient and you crave a whole host of red marks in your diary. This collector's approach can be found in books, too. You could, like the Famous Five, seek out castles, or get lost in a series of fabulous E. Nesbit-style mazes, or look for the kinds of secret and walled gardens that feature in Frances Hodgson Burnett's stories. This way, it's possible to have the best of both worlds: something to plan with pleasure and something to savour afterwards. These children in books, they know a thing or two about enjoying themselves.

10 GREAT LITERARY SPOTS TO VISIT WITH A BOOK

Here are a few ideas for literary days out with a book in hand.

1. Famous Five books: visit Corfe Castle and the surrounding area. Pack a picnic, hire bicycles, clamber up to the castle and look for smugglers.

2. Five Find-Outer books: enjoy an autumnal walk or bike ride in Burnham Beeches followed by a Fatty-style tea in a tea shop.

3. Swallows and Amazons series: take a trip on the steamer or hire a rowing boat on Lake Coniston, drink hot tea and eat local toffee.

4. Anne of Green Gables books: take a trip to Prince Edward Island, Canada, where there's a whole tourist industry set up around L.M. Montgomery's books and innumerable things to see and do

5. Paddington Bear stories: browse the antiques shops on Portobello Road and enjoy an elevenses of cocoa and a posh bun from the Hummingbird Bakery (133 Portobello Road www.hummingbirdbakery.com).

6. *The Wind in the Willows*: take a hamper full of food and mess about in boats on the Thames near Henley and Pangbourne.

7. *Winnie-the-Pooh*: go to Ashdown Forest to play Poohsticks (see page 109) and look for heffalumps.

8. *The Saturdays*: visit an art gallery in Manhattan then enjoy afternoon tea in a smart hotel.

9. *Ballet Shoes*: take the Underground to Knightsbridge, walk along the Cromwell Road looking in the shop windows and visit the Victoria and Albert Museum.

10. *The Family from One End Street*: take a bus, or drive, from Lewes ('Otwell' in the books) to Brighton, have a paddle, saunter up and down the promenade and eat fish and chips.

Find Your Way Round a Maze

CHILDREN FIND MAZES STRANGELY and powerfully fascinating. And while for some the idea of deliberately getting lost in a huge puzzle in order to find their way out again is terrifying, for others it's incredibly exciting.

Gerald in E. Nesbit's *The Enchanted Castle* is most definitely in the latter category. He sees a maze as an adventure, and is unperturbed by the idea that he might meet something scary in the middle and possibly never come out again. Indeed, he is thrilled when at the start of their potentially dull summer holidays at school he, Jimmy and Kathleen come upon a wonderful, magical garden which, they have heard, surrounds an enchanted castle.

"Beyond the rose garden was a yew hedge with an arch cut in it, and it was the beginning of a maze like the one at Hampton Court.

'Now,' said Gerald, 'you mark my words. In the middle of this maze we shall find the secret enchantment. Draw your swords, my merry men all, and hark forward tallyho in the utmost silence.'

Which they did."

Four attempts later they find themselves once again at the rose arch and Jimmy is ready to turn back. Nonsense, thinks Gerald.

"'Let's have one more try at the maze. I hate giving things up,' said Gerald."

It's at this moment that they spot a red thread tied to a thimble and Gerald declares it's a clue, so they follow it "and it was a clue, and it led right into the middle of the maze. And in the very middle of the maze they come upon the wonder", a bejewelled, enchanted princess, and they truly believe they have walked "right into the middle of a fairy-tale".

✒ PRACTICAL ✒

➡ There are hedge mazes, mirror mazes, panel mazes, maize mazes, mosaic and paving mazes, and turf mazes all over Great Britain. The most famous maze is at Hampton Court, the largest is at York and the longest is at Longleat.

➡ Each summer there are numerous temporary maize mazes in the United Kingdom, created in conjunction with farmers. For information, look at www.maizemaze.com.

➡ Most mazes now have a way of helping visitors to find their way out if they panic or feel very lost. Some have a look-out person in a high chair to guide people out, others let groups carry flags in order to follow systems, and others have raised viewing platforms and bridges.

➡ There are also plenty of maze activities that can be explored without getting lost. Many children enjoy doing maze puzzles on paper; there masses of these can be printed off the internet. Or buy books of maze puzzles.

HOW TO MAKE YOUR OWN MAZE

☂ Create small-scale model mazes, for example, with Jenga bricks, dominoes, bricks and books and put play people in them.

☂ Make pebble mazes on a beach.

☂ Use chalks to create chalk mazes on pavements.

☂ Design your own maze. See Jo Edkins' maze page for all sorts of maze information and design ideas:
http://gwydir.demon.co.uk/jo/maze/design/index.htm

'Own' a Castle

IMAGINE YOU ARE CYCLING THROUGH the English countryside. The sun is shining, villages with thatched cottages are dotted all around, the sea glitters in the distance, the hedgerows are full of flowers and fruit, and there's a gentle breeze. You wheel round a corner and there in front of you is a tall mound with a spectacular, ancient, ruined castle perched on top. Imagine the surprise and thrill of coming face to face with such a castle for the first time, a castle that conjures up wonderful stories and images of battles, romances, attacks and sieges, dungeons and dragons, lords, ladies and peasants.

This is exactly what it's like when you encounter the marvellously atmospheric Corfe Castle in Dorset. No wonder Enid Blyton took it as the prototype for Kirrin Castle, moved it to an island (Kirrin Island) for even greater mystery and visual impact, and used it as an unforgettable setting or backdrop for so many of her Famous Five stories.

Like all good ruined castles, Kirrin/Corfe Castle sets the imagination alight and creates all sorts of adventurous possibilities and narratives in the minds of visitors. Well-maintained castles with roofs and interiors and furnishings are fantastic, but they don't allow for the roaming of children's feet and imaginations as they climb up towers, walk along walls, leap from piles of tumbledown stones, peer through arrow slits and lean over parapets. And while ruined castles do not offer pre-packaged history, they do invite a far more personal interpretation and are exciting places to explore and act out stories and fantasies.

They are not too grand or too perfect or too crowded, and there is always the possibility of meeting birds and bats and other unusual occupants. Ruined castles are also ideal locations from which to watch the sun set or the moon rise, and they are fabulously evocative at any time of year (snow-covered ruins are particularly beautiful).

I think everyone should have a castle of their own ('mine' has always been the precipitous Peveril Castle in the Peak District). Not that we can all be like George in the Famous Five books who really does own the deeds to Kirrin Castle; but we can all climb up an escarpment or mound to our favourite castle, reach the top, survey our kingdom and utter the words every child loves to say, 'I'm the king of the castle'.

PRACTICAL

I admit to having a passion for castles, particularly the ruined sort.

These are my favourite ruined castles:

* Conwy, North Wales
* Urquhart, Invernesshire
* Peveril, Derbyshire
* Pevensey, Sussex
* Goodrich, Herefordshire
* Kenilworth, Warwickshire
* Skipton, Yorkshire
* Orford, Suffolk
* Framlingham, Suffolk
* Berkhamsted, Hertfordshire

And these are the castles that are on my to-be-visited list:

* Bolingbroke, Lincolnshire
* Camber, Sussex
* Egremont, Cumbria
* Kendal, Cumbria
* Pickering, Yorkshire
* Richmond, Yorkshire
* Rochester, Kent
* Tintagel, Cornwall
* Ludlow, Shropshire
* Brougham, Cumbria

Have a Day at the Seaside

I'VE ALWAYS HAD A SOFT SPOT FOR stories in which children get terrifically and wildly excited when they catch their first glimpse of the sea on a special day out or at the beginning of a holiday. From Josie Smith in Magdalen Nabb's *Josie Smith in Summer* who can barely contain herself, to the Famous Five who are never, ever blasé about arriving at the seaside (though goodness knows they've been there enough), to Eve Garnett's *Family from One End Street* for whom a day at the seaside is the best treat imaginable.

The family live just a six-mile bus ride away from the east coast, but getting there isn't easy when there are seven mouths to feed and no spare cash. But Mr Ruggles is determined they should have "a good Blow Out on Bank Holidays" and takes extra jobs to finance an August Bank Holiday trip to the seaside each year. And once they are there, they have a wonderful time enjoying all the things you should enjoy at the seaside: tea and buns, walking along the promenade, a dinner of pork pies and doughnuts and bananas on the beach, fun on the pier, listening to a band and laughing at the pierrots, paddling and, the highlight of the day, a special tea of fish and chips or "shrimps and cockles and other delicacies" in one of the seafront shanties.

Such is their capacity for enjoyment, they even manage to make the most of wet bank holidays, putting more affluent readers who grumble about this great British institution to shame:

"Even a wet Bank Holiday was enjoyable at Brightwell, for the day could be spent under cover in the Amusement Arcade with sometimes a finish up at the Cinema."

In many ways, this and all the other seaside stories remind us that in order to embrace and appreciate the great British seaside it's best to retain an element of playfulness and childishness. It's no good going there all grumpy and miserable and cynical; you need to go the way children in books go – with buckets and spades, swimming costumes and towels, blankets and picnics, ready to dig furiously, eat for England, make new friends and have adventures.

RIPPING THINGS TO DO AT THE SEASIDE:

- Saunter along the pier and play on slot machines.
- Eat fish and chips in a chippy or café or share them with the seagulls on the beach.
- Enjoy ice creams, sticks of rock, and sweets in the shapes of prawns and shells and false teeth.
- Mark chalk dots on pebbles and play dominoes, make pebble mazes, write your name in pebbles, skim pebbles on the sea to see who can get the most 'bounces'.

➤ Make sandcastles, dig a hole to Australia, dig for treasure, bury siblings and parents in the sand.

➤ Hire deckchairs by the bandstand and listen to the band play.

➤ Have a *Josie Smith at the Seaside* day out with sandy sandwiches, donkey rides, handstands, sandcastles and windmills.

➤ Have a *Ballet Shoes* Sussex coast day out. The three Fossil sisters have a marvellous time when they stay at Pevensey Bay, doing exercises on the beach, enjoying trips to Eastbourne and afternoon tea at Beachy Head. After all this time (the book was first published in 1936) this is still a lovely bit of seaside for families.

➤ Swim in the sea.

➤ Go beachcombing at low tide at any time of year.

Chases and Trails

ALTHOUGH IT MAY NOT BE ACCEPTABLE these days to drop trails of paper over the countryside, the principle of the paperchase or following a trail is an idea still worth exploiting, and there's no shortage of literary inspiration.

Think of the timeless myths and fairy tales that tell of safe returns by means of simple trails: Theseus finding his way out of the Minotaur's labyrinth using nothing more than a ball of thread, or Hansel and Gretel dropping breadcrumbs to lead them back home after they have been abandoned by their wicked stepmother (a plan that is foiled by hungry birds). Or the Rugby School hare and hounds chase in *Tom Brown's Schooldays*, or the hearty college paperchase that is so wonderfully and breathlessly described by Judy in one of her letters in Jean Webster's *Daddy-Long-Legs*? And who could ever forget the grammar school boys' paperchase that Bobbie, Peter and Phyllis watch in E. Nesbit's *The Railway Children* and the drama that ensues?

It's the thrill of the chase, the excitement of the hunt that makes paperchases and trails so irresistible. But they don't all have to be large scale and cross-country and the basic idea can be adapted to suit more confined spaces and younger children.

PRACTICAL

All the following chases and trails rely on the 'hares' (one or two) leaving a 'scent' that the 'hounds' can follow, which is why the some people call a paperchase 'hare and hounds'.

➡ In a traditional paperchase a couple of hares set off with a canvas shoulder bag filled with scraps of paper, for example, newspaper, which they scatter as they run, making false trails, detours and U-turns to confuse the hounds and put them off the scent. After an interval of a few minutes, the hounds set off on the chase. If the hare makes it to the finishing line first, he chooses the next hare. If not, the hound who catches him chooses the next hare.

➡ If you have younger children, a trail or paperchase works just as well in a garden or in the house. Utilise all the space you have and place trails round shrubs and trees, up and down stairs, in and out of cupboards and round furniture. Of course, the trail could be a series of clues which turns the game into a treasure hunt.

➡ An urban version of a paperchase uses chalk marks on pavements and walls and is easy for children themselves to organise on a residential street or housing estate.

➡ Or adapt the idea for an Easter egg hunt. Draw little rabbit footprints on paper and cut them out (if you have a photocopier it's easy to copy extra sheets). Get up early on Easter Sunday and place the bunny prints in a trail round the house and/or garden that goes past small eggs hidden in nooks and crannies, and leads eventually to a large egg. Give each child a little basket, bag or bowl for collecting the treats.

➡ Children are fascinated by the trail of breadcrumbs left by Hansel and Gretel in the forest. So why not let them do same in the garden? It's a good way of using stale bread and feeding birds at the same time. And when the children come back inside safely, perhaps they could have some gingerbread?

Treasure Hunting

THERE CAN BE FEW MORE POTENT themes in children's books than that of hidden treasure. Looking for and unearthing a heavy chest of glittering coins or a huge cache of sparkling jewels, solid gold ingots, priceless paintings or stolen silverware is at the heart of countless thrilling tales. Throw in maps and clues, pirates and smugglers, red herrings and wild goose chases, plus the possibility of being rich beyond one's wildest dreams, and it's no wonder it's a formula that has been worked and reworked over and over again.

The idea of finding or stumbling upon treasure is one that permeates children's ordinary lives, too. They believe with touching faith that unheard of wealth *can* be found by chance or by following clues, that rags to riches stories *do* come true, and that there's a high possibility of finding treasure in any back garden or on any beach. And this is why organised treasure hunts are perennially popular: they guarantee that treasure will be found. Plus, children are always happy to practise looking for it, because they know that the world is full of undiscovered treasure.

 **PRACTICAL**

There are several types of treasure hunt. The first is the *Treasure Island* version which follows cryptic clues (and sometimes a map) until the treasure is located. The second is simply a matter of finding treasure hidden in various spots by searching a given area. And the third is looking for a set list of items or 'treasure'. In all cases, winners and finders are rewarded with a piece of

195

treasure: money, sweets, chocolate or whatever you care to call treasure.

Treasure Island hunt: suitable for older children or children working in pairs. To be a success, this type of treasure hunt requires a fair degree planning and organisation. Draw up a map to show the location of the clues, or set and hide clues that lead on from each other. Devise clever/cryptic clues that test the hunters' knowledge of the location or their general knowledge or powers of observation.

Hidden treasure: this is easy and great fun. Hide treasure in various spots around the house or garden or the hunt location (if necessary, make a note of where you have put it – it's very easy to forget). When our children were young, we used to do three variations of this type of hunt: one in wherever we were staying on holiday, making the most of the unusual location, one for Easter and one for Hallowe'en. The last was the highlight of Phoebe's birthday party: we hid treasure around the garden, waited till it was dark, gave every child a torch (very cheap from hardware stores and they doubled as the 'going home' present) and let them loose outside.

Treasure gathering: this is a great way to make the most of being outside, in the park, going for a walk or spending time at the beach. Make a list of 'treasure' to be collected by the hunters, who can seek individually or in teams, and either hand out the lists or call out what has to be found. The first team/person to collect everything is the winner. On a walk, treasure could be: certain types of leaves (by tree type, colour), conkers, acorns, fir cones, insects, feathers, pickable flowers such as daisies or buttercups in the wild, pieces of moss, something beginning with a certain letter. In your garden it could be balls, certain garden flowers (by name, colour), fruits, leaves (by type, colour, smell, for example, lavender or mint), ten pieces of gravel, a lost shoes, fallen branches, seeds, pets. On a beach, set children looking for: certain shapes and colours of pebbles, sea glass, shells, dead fish, pieces of orange rope, seaweed, lolly sticks, something that sinks/floats. Children also enjoy digging for treasure, like the Bastables in E. Nesbit's *The Story of the Treasure Seekers* who dig a huge hole in their back garden (many parents may prefer major hole-digging to be done at the beach). They also like "Turnupstuffing" as Astrid Lindgren's Pippi Longstocking calls it, which is general foraging and poking about looking for what some people would call rubbish and others might call treasure. Turnupstuffing is a great way of adding interest to a walk. When it's done on a beach it becomes beachcombing.

Have a Birthday Picnic

THERE ARE ALL SORTS OF LOVELY BIRTHDAY treats and cakes in
children's books because birthday treats and cakes are some of the most
important things in the world when you are young. One of the loveliest of all,
one that must cause pangs of envy in every reader, is Petrova's birthday picnic
in Noel Streatfeild's *Ballet Shoes*.

It's summer so all the guests pile into two cars and drive from London to a
wood near Westerham in Kent. They enjoy a "terrific meal from Fortnum and
Mason's" for lunch, and eat so much they can't do anything except lie on the
pine needles and look at the sun coming through the tree and feel "absolutely
contented". Later, Posy takes off her shoes and does a little dance for each of
them, miming what they do and making them all laugh; the three girls make
vows to put the Fossil name in history books then play hide-and-seek until tea
which is a "gorgeous affair".

Since money is short in their household, Petrova doesn't have any proper
presents, but "a pink-and-white birthday cake with her name on it, and
candles, was a great comfort", as is the gold half-sovereign she discovers in her
slice. The birthday celebrations conclude in great style with a box of daylight
fireworks, and the girls make a little monument with a used firework to mark
the spot where they spent Petrova's birthday.

It's a perfect day and a perfect inspiration for all sorts of special birthday
picnics.

PRACTICAL

- It would be rather splendid to order a Fortnum and Mason hamper for your picnic, but sadly this is beyond the budget of most of us. However, an old-fashioned wicker hamper still feels very special even if you have had to fill it yourself. Consider borrowing one (plenty of people still have one stashed away in the loft or garage) or buying one from somewhere like Picnic Shop www.picnicshop.co.uk or John Lewis. If it's true, Great-British-picnic style you want, look for wonderful vintage wicker hampers for sale on eBay or in flea markets.

- Or make your own picnic and include lots of favourite treats. The trick is to keep it simple – a picnic should be an enjoyable affair, not a military operation.

- Bring extras and entertainment according to the tastes of the birthday boy or girl and the season, for example, balls, games, music, candles or lights, fireworks, matches, small barbecue, primus stove, rugs, folding chairs.

- Do not be put off if a birthday doesn't fall in summer. There are possibilities for picnics all year round as long as you cater accordingly, wrap up well, and organise warming activities and games. Think soup, hot potatoes, toffee and mulled wine when it's cold, or filled baguettes, fruit and hot chocolate when it's milder.

Amazing Adventures

IF THERE'S ONE THING CHILDREN'S BOOKS can be relied on to deliver, it's adventure. Indeed, the adventure story is acknowledged as a genre in its own right with a long, illustrious and action-packed history in which the likes of Robinson Crusoe and Biggles rub shoulders with Jim Hawkins in *Treasure Island* and Alex Rider, in tales that make the reader's heart rate soar and the pages turn faster and faster.

In all adventure books, whether they are of the kidnapping, treasure-hunting, death-defying variety or fall into the summer holiday, boats and kites category, one message comes over loud and clear: life itself is an amazing adventure. All you have to do is emulate your favourite adventurers and embrace new challenges, throw yourself into new experiences, use all your energy and skills to push yourself and adventure will come to meet you. And if children can't set off alone like Huckleberry Finn and Tom Sawyer, or rely on their parents disappearing in school holidays like so many of Enid Blyton's characters, they can still take the elements of adventure (tents, campfires, outdoor living, maps, expeditions and plenty of food) and have their very own home-grown variety.

For the more timid or cautious readers, adventure books offer a huge vicarious thrill and an adrenalin rush that might be enough to satisfy their cravings for excitement. And if the reader is fearless, daring and ready to be tested, then books contain all the ideas he or she will ever need for amazing adventures, from sailing in coracles to arctic adventures, from sleeping in home-made tents to roasting pigs' tails over a campfire.

Discover the joys of coracles

TREASURE ISLAND BY ROBERT LOUIS STEVENSON is one of those classic books that everyone thinks they have read but mostly haven't; yet we all know it's the ultimate tale of adventure and pirates, buccaneers and buried gold, maps and quests and hiding in apple barrels, grotesque characters and squawking parrots.

And then, of course, there's the coracle in the chapter 'The Cruise of the Coracle'. This is the little one-man boat in which our hero, the young Jim Hawkins, approaches the *Hispaniola* (the frigate packed with mutineers) to cut it adrift and sever their hopes of getting the treasure. In the midst of all the drama and excitement of this part of the story, it occurred to me that Jim's "sea-tossed coracle" is a most brilliant boat for adventurous children to sail in.

It is "home-made if anything was home-made; a rude, lop-sided framework of tough wood, and stretched upon that a covering of goat-skin, with the hair inside", plus a "thwart" and a double paddle. It's described as "such a thing as ancient Britons made", and it's true — when the Romans invaded Britain, they found many a Briton bouncing about and fishing on rivers and streams in what looked like large upturned walnut shells. It is "exceedingly light and portable" (it can be carried on a person's back like a tortoise's shell) and noiseless and therefore perfect for Jim's sabotage work. And it's also marvellously seaworthy.

Amazingly enough, the coracle is still around today. It's such a clever design that it is used for night-time fishing and eel-catching on shallow streams and rivers in Wales, Shropshire and the Fens. And it is still the ideal boat for a young adventurer: it's buoyant, light, and once the way it bobs and spins on the water has been mastered, it is easy to manage. It's like a safer, more solid version of the inflatable dinghy and just as much fun on the water.

 **PRACTICAL**

➜ Look at http://www.coraclemaker.co.uk/ if you are interested in buying a traditional coracle. Alternatively, you can buy instructions for making one for £5 or attend a coracle-making course.

➜ Green Wood Centre runs coracle-making courses: www.greenwoodcentre.org.uk.

➜ You can find free instructions for making a coracle on the internet.

➜ If you want to watch people racing in coracles and find out more about these boats, go to one of the coracle regattas held in England and Wales each summer. Use Google to find up-to-date details.

➜ Inflatable dinghies are the obvious alternative to coracles, but I would stress the need for constant caution and surveillance when children use them.

Heroic Exploits

CHILDREN NEED HEROES. Not only do they need heroes for stories of indomitable human spirit, incredible acts of bravery and the desire to conquer, they also need heroes to inspire their games.

Just think how many children have followed in their heroes' footsteps and walked on the moon, flown countless bombing raids, played at Lord's/ Wembley/Twickenham, raced to the North or South Pole and commanded entire armies. And how many, in their imagination, have scaled the mountains of Switzerland and climbed Everest? Well, I'd say plenty, but not very many as realistically as Richmal Crompton's William Brown in 'William and White Satin'.

The early William stories were written and published at a time when the Swiss Alpine Club was in full swing and George Mallory (1886–1924) was taking part in the first three British expeditions to Mount Everest. So when William is given an old alpenstock (Alpine walking-stick) what else does he decide to do but use it to climb mountains? He and the Outlaws set up a plank against the garden wall and scramble up it, "roped together and wearing feathers in their caps. William was wearing an old golf cap of his mother's and mentally pictured himself as an impressive and heroic figure."

But William is soon to be outdone in the matter of domestic mountaineering by, horror of horrors, a girl (proving that girls, like boys, need heroes, and not just heroines). Dorita dismisses his idea of mountaineering: "You're a mug... I know a mountaineering game worth ten of that old thing.'" Using her version, she and William take the mattresses from four beds, lay them on the stairs and nail them to the stairs to "secure the stability of the 'mountain'". They then put all the pillows and bolsters they can find at the bottom and proceed to scramble up their stair-mountain by digging the point of the alpenstock into the mattresses then slipping and tumbling down to land in a heap on the pillows.

When he reaches the summit, William pauses and considers his position. "He was well aware that retribution was not far off… but he cared for none of these things… a smile of triumph curved his lips." And if asked why he had done it, he would no doubt have uttered the immortal words attributed to his hero George Mallory: 'Because it was there'.

⚬⚬ PRACTICAL ⚬⚬

■→ Now, I'm not for one minute suggesting that children should be encouraged to drag mattresses off beds and nail them to staircases in a search for an authentic mountaineering experience, but William's imaginative interpretation of heroic deeds shows that children will always want to hear of great feats and of great heroes and heroines, and then be inspired to interpret these stories imaginatively and creatively.

■→ It also tells me that children's logic is impeccable (mattresses are the perfect, slippery surface and stairs the perfect angled peak) but that their thinking is far removed from adult thinking. So when you see something utterly bizarre happening in your house, the first question is *what* they are doing and not *why* the mattresses/pillows/clothes/kitchen contents are all over the place. The answer may be surprisingly heroic.

■→ The stories and tales of great heroes and heroines are still in print. A library is possibly the best place to look as they keep these kinds of books for school projects.

Have an Arctic Adventure

FROM CAPTAIN SCOTT, ROALD AMUNDSEN, Ernest Shackleton and
Fridtjof Nansen to Ranulph Fiennes and David Hempelman-Adams, famous
polar explorers have fascinated generations of children. Theirs is a history of
amazing characters and dazzling stories of daring and heroic exploits, survival
and death, tragedy and triumph, and even today it exerts a remarkable pull on the
collective imagination. We lap up accounts of those uninhabited, inhospitable,
frozen lands that demand phenomenal strength of mind and purpose of their
explorers, and these stories still inspire the children who hear them, just as they
inspired the children in Arthur Ransome's *Winter Holiday*, written in 1940.

The Swallows and Amazons, plus newcomers Dick and Dorothea, need to
fill a potentially dreary, empty winter holiday in the Lake District, so they
decide to start a polar expedition. But when they are forced to remain there in
quarantine for several weeks longer than they had expected, the expedition
becomes ever more elaborate and daring, and closer to the real thing. They
take all the details they can find of famous expeditions such as Nansen's
voyages to the North Pole in the *Fram*, and weave them into their adventure. So
they march across a "frozen sea", set up a race to the North Pole, live on
Captain Flint's boat which is stuck in ice (they rename it the *Fram* after
Nansen's boat which became ice-bound on his 1893 expedition). They travel
with sledges and pretend to be the dogs pulling them, they ski and skate, and
eat explorers' "pemmican". They are faithful to historical accounts to the very
end, when they finally reach the North Pole (a flagstaff in a wooden lakeside
shelter) in a raging blizzard.

It's a humdinger of a story, full of energy and clever ideas and a certain British pluckiness, guaranteed to satisfy and inspire any young polar explorer, armchair or real.

PRACTICAL

An arctic adventure is one of those games like climbing mountains or being shipwrecked that have their origins in exciting stories and true histories. Children take the germ of an idea and develop it in often strange and wonderful ways, and don't actually need frozen wastes, mountains and wrecked ships to make their adventure seem real. So while snow and ice are a bonus and certainly add authenticity, it's possible to organise a race to the North Pole or a spell on an ice-bound ship anywhere, even indoors. Here are some ideas for an arctic adventure, many of which come from *Winter Holiday*.

OUTDOOR EXPEDITIONS

- If you are having a race to the North or South Pole or a polar exploration, use a stick or bamboo cane to mark the position of the pole you are aiming to reach.
- Make a map and plot the best route.
- Create teams and, like Captain Scott and Roald Amundsen, have a race to the South Pole. (You could change history and let Scott and his men win.)
- Dress in explorers' outfits with snow goggles and anoraks or parkas, gloves and balaclavas or close-fitting hats.
- Use sledges and toboggans and pretend you are British explorers who either 'man-hauled' or pulled their sledges themselves or used horses. Or

use a piece of thick plastic or heavy-duty bin bags that will slide easily over the ground as a pretend sledge.

- Get out any skiing equipment you may have (skis, sticks, goggles, clothes, boots) and pretend to be Norwegian explorers who skied to the South Pole while their dogs pulled the sledges. If you don't have skis, tie tennis rackets to your feet and plod across the 'ice'.

- If there is snow, build an igloo or snow den. If not, make a pretend one.

- Or put up a tent and keep warm and sheltered inside.

- Take plenty of food and drink. Polar explorers eat biscuits and pemmican (a mix of dried meat and fat packed into tins – corned beef is a good substitute) and drink hot cocoa in their tents and igloos. Biscuits similar to the ones Scott and his men took to the South Pole have recently been launched: Captain Scott's Expedition Biscuits are made by Huntley & Palmers, one of the companies that sponsored his 1911–12 expedition.

- Use signals and codes to communicate with the rest of the party.

INDOOR EXPEDITIONS

- Plan your route or march. Draw up a map. Set up a pole to reach (a sweeping brush, a piece of furniture, a bedpost with a flag tied to it).

- A settee, chair or bed can be Antarctica or the North or South Pole, or a ship stuck in ice.

- Get out any stuffed penguins you may have if you are travelling to the South Pole, white polar bears if you are going to the North Pole.

- Use walking sticks, golf clubs, umbrellas for snow sticks and sunglasses for snow goggles, and dress in exploring outfits: balaclavas, parkas, anoraks and gloves.

- Make a tent or igloo with white sheets, pillows and uncovered duvets.
- Or use the sheets/pillows/duvets as snow/ice floes/frozen wastes.
- Use magazines and walking sticks to ski on the carpet, and sleeping bags or bin bags as sledges/toboggans.
- Take pemmican and biscuits (see Outdoor Expeditions) and ask the cook to make hot cocoa and Igloo Hotpot (see page 238) for when you return to base camp.
- You may need your signalling skills (see page 17) in case you get stuck in the snow or attacked by a polar bear or king penguin.

Be Prepared...

... BECAUSE, AS ENID BLYTON POINTS out in *Five Go to Smuggler's Top*, "Adventures always come to the adventurous, there's no doubt about that!"

Even though most children can't experience for themselves many of the ripping adventures boys and girls in books enjoy, they can always be ready for them. Indeed, many spend their childhood inspired by fictional exploits and privately preparing for an adventure by making lists and practising their skills, so that should one some day come their way they are ready to leap into action like any well-drilled boy scout.

You can, of course, draw up your own list of what you need in order to be prepared for adventure, or you can take tips from the professionals – so here are some shining examples of being prepared:

HOW TO PREPARE FOR AN ADVENTURE

→ In *Five Get Into Trouble* the children plan for a carefree cycling holiday which turns into a kidnapping adventure. So it's just as well they have bikes, tents, maps, rucksacks and food with them.

→ In *Five On a Hike Together* they prepare for a half-term hiking weekend by packing socks, barley sugar and a large-scale map of the moors between their two schools – all of which is useful in the adventure that unfolds.

→ In *Five Run Away Together* they do exactly that, and take all they need to survive a long stay on Kirrin Island: dozens of tins of food and bottles of ginger beer, containers of fresh water, methylated spirits for the stove, candles, lots of rugs and cushions, a bone for Timmy the dog.

➤ The Swallows in Arthur Ransome's *Swallows and Amazons* make a list of all they'll need on the back of the telegram from their father that says they can go off on their own. It includes a compass, kettle, flag, telescope, saucepan, mugs, knives, forks, tea, sugar, milk, spoons and a large seed cake.

➤ They also go well prepared with reading matter: Susan takes *Simple Cooking for Small Households*, Titty takes *Robinson Crusoe* and John packs *The Seaman's Handybook* and Part Three of *The Baltic Pilot*

➤ Fatty in the Five Find-Outer books fills his pockets with tons of things that might just be useful. He carries an orange so that he can write an SOS message in invisible ink and a small roll of wire for picking locks, toffees for sustenance, matchboxes for collecting clues and plenty of cash for cakes, buns, lemonade and ice creams.

This is my checklist for a basic, essential adventure kit that can be used on hikes, camping trips, holidays and weekend outings:

* Tents; rucksack, torch and compass
* Maps including star maps (see page 31)
* Plenty of food, and campfire cooking and toasting skills
* Fire-lighting skills and matches
* Binoculars ('field-glasses' as in so many Enid Blyton stories)
* Signalling skills, and equipment such as mirrors and torches for flashing, and flags for semaphore
* Matchboxes for keeping clues in
* A length of rope and a ball of string
* Own flag (optional unless you are planning a *Swallows and Amazons*-style adventure in which case it is vital)
* Books: bird-watching and nature guides, and a basic cookery book

Make a Rope Swing

"MR ZUCKERMAN HAD THE BEST SWING in the county. It was a single long piece of heavy rope tied to a beam... at the bottom of the rope was a fat knot to sit on. It was arranged so that you could swing without being pushed. You climbed a ladder to the hayloft. Then, holding the rope, you stood at the edge... then you straddled the knot, so that it acted as a seat... then you got up all your nerve... and jumped."

Few families have a huge barn with what looks like a twenty-foot drop (see illustration) in which to swing, but there can't be many children who don't love the sensation of sailing and twisting and turning and zooming through the air. It's one of those things that is guaranteed to make the onlooker feel more terrified than the person doing it; the child gets the adrenalin rush while any adults watching get the burden of acute anxiety.

If you're still nervous about the idea of children and swings, consider what E.B. White says in *Charlotte's Web*. He makes the excellent and very astute observation that the vast majority of children have absolutely no intention of not holding on tightly, and that children do not get on a swing with the express aim of falling off and hurting themselves (in fact, the only time they let go deliberately is to land in water or bales of hay).

"Mothers from miles around worried about Zuckerman's swing. They feared some child would fall off. But no child ever did. Children almost always hold on to things tighter than their parents think they will."

E.B. White recognises that the stomach-churning joys of swings create some of the best moments of childhood, and that you don't need much in

order to get the best out of the concept. Some space, a rope, a high beam or strong branch are enough, and if these happen to be over something soft to land on or a stream or pool to fall in, then it's all the better for everyone, swinger and spectators alike.

Swim Outdoors

THERE WAS A TIME, IN SUMMERS gone by, when children's first and most natural reaction on seeing a body of water was to run down to its edge, strip off and leap in, squeal and swim, and generally have a wonderful time. Just as the Famous Five so often do.

There's a fine example of their contagious enthusiasm for outdoor swimming in *Five Run Away Together*. Julian, Dick, Anne and George have run away to Kirrin Island and wake up on their first morning with a great sense of excitement. They put the kettle on to boil and go in search of somewhere to swim before breakfast:

"'Look! There's a simply marvellous pool in the middle of those rocks over there!' called Julian, pointing. 'We've never spotted it before. Golly, it's like a small swimming pool made, specially for us!'

'Kirrin Swimming Pool...' said Dick... 'Come on it looks gorgeous!'"

In they all go, diving and splashing and swimming and floating, before racing back to their cave for a nice hot drink and a hearty breakfast, all ready and energised for whatever adventure awaits.

🥨 PRACTICAL 🥨

Today we are a lot more cautious (sometimes too cautious), but it's still possible to enjoy the exhilaration and exuberance of outdoor swimming that Enid Blyton manages to capture so perfectly. We just need to break out of overheated, overcrowded, overbossy pools and swim the way nature intended –

outdoors and under the sky. There is nothing like seeing the world from water level.

➤ The United Kingdom is full of amazing places to swim. Some are obvious, others are not; to find them, consult www.wildswimming.co.uk and www.outdoorswimmingsociety.com.

➤ There are campaigns to save lidos up and down the country, but the best way to do this is to use them. Look at www.lidos.org.uk to find out what's near you.

NOTE: Some lidos are heated and open all year round.

➤ Find your own exclusive swimming place. It's not difficult – outdoor swimmers often have whole beaches or pools or rivers to themselves.

➤ Or simply brace yourself and go for a swim in the sea.

The Importance of Tents

WE ALL KNOW CAMPING IS COOL these days. We read about designer tents and smart campsites in the travel and lifestyle sections of newspapers. We discover that camping is eco-everything (including economical), and we believe we have discovered the Next Big Thing.

Well, I hate to break it to you, but camping has always been cool. You only have to have read the books of Enid Blyton and Arthur Ransome and many other twentieth-century writers to know this is true; they confirm camping is marvellous and tents are brilliant.

In fact, it's clear in the books that these temporary canvas homes are the most alluring aspect of the whole camping experience. How enticing is the thought of crawling in, closing the flaps, listening to the wind and the wildlife? Or sticking your head out to look at the night sky while your body stays warm in a sleeping bag? Or playing cards by the light of a torch? Or telling ghost stories in the dark?

It's possible to make a tent using Arthur Ransome's practical, detailed description of how mother makes tents out of thin canvas for the children's adventures in *Swallows and Amazons*. This is how she does it:

"The tents were of the simplest kind. Each tent had a three-cornered piece for the back. The back was sewn to the sides, and a piece of stout rope was stitched to the canvas inside to make the ridge of the roof. The ends of this rope were fastened to two trees, and so held the tent up. No tent poles were needed. Along the bottom of the back and sides were big pockets, to be filled with stones. On the rocky ground, where you cannot drive in tent pegs, this is

a good plan. At the front of the tent there were loose flaps, joined to the sides, so that they could be rolled up and tied out of the way."

All that's needed now is a groundsheet, some haybags, rugs and blankets, and "you'll come to no harm", as Mother says to Roger. To which, if he was around today, his reply would undoubtedly be 'Cool'.

PRACTICAL

It helps if you know someone like Mother who can run up a tent, but not everyone does. However, all is not lost. As John says in *Swallows and Amazons*, it's possible to make a very simple tent "out of a sail by hanging it across the [boat's] yard for a ridge pole, and... [holding it up] with two pairs of oars, a pair at each end".

❧ Alternatively, landlocked and garden campers can tie a length of rope between two trees and drape a piece of canvas (or a sheet or a curtain or a blanket) over it to make a very rudimentary tent. Or they can use a washing line and hold the fabric in place with stones. A waterproof sheet or rug makes a difference at any time of year, and keeps blankets, rugs, duvets, pillows, cushions and everything else that is dragged out of the house dry and relatively clean.

❧ Or you can erect a real tent in the garden and let children play in it, use it as a changing room or performance area for circuses and shows and sleep in it. It's the ultimate holiday-at-home activity.

❧ Indoor tents are great fun, too. They can be made from sheets and blankets draped over furniture and tables, with piles of books to hold the sides taut.

❧ Every camper should have a torch for finding their way around in the dark, reading books, making shadow puppets, putting on light shows, and making silhouettes to amuse others outside the tent.

❧ If you want a family camping holiday with a difference (the tents remind me of the *Little House on the Prairie* illustrations) look at the Feather Down Farm Days site www.featherdown.co.uk.

Enjoy the Heavens Above

SLEEPING OUTSIDE IS ONE OF THOSE amazing adventures that children enjoy in books set in Australia, America and India. Descriptions of exotic verandas, balconies and roof terraces, balmy nights, starlit skies and buzzing insects make many young readers yearn to drag their bedding outside and sleep with nothing between them and the heavens.

Despite its far from tropical climate, even in Britain the idea is not unthinkable and there are sometimes nights that are perfect for sleeping out. All that is needed to enjoy the sights, smells and sounds of a summer's night is the forecast of warmth and dryness, a sleeping bag, and a measure of Pollyanna-ish spontaneity.

When Pollyanna, heroine of the novel of the same name by Eleanor H. Porter, comes to live with her uncompromising Aunt Polly, her bedroom is a bare attic with its windows fastened tight for fear of letting in flies. One night she goes up to bed to find her room as hot as an oven, so she finds a window she can open, happily breathes in the fresh air, notices that the sun parlour below has a wide, flat roof and immediately wishes her bed were out there.

Several bags holding winter clothes are being stored in the attic, and she takes one containing a sealskin coat for a bed and two thin bags for a pillow and a cover. She climbs out of the window, rejoicing in the cool and refreshing air and, with a sigh of content, settles down to sleep. Unfortunately, her nocturnal adventure is interrupted by those indoors who fear a burglar is creeping about on the roof. But Pollyanna's exploitation of a beautiful night is all that is needed to plant in the reader's mind the idea that sleeping rough is not rough at all, but is in fact wonderfully exciting.

PRACTICAL

➤ Choose a warm, dry night but make it easy to retire indoors should the temperature drop or rain fall, or if anyone becomes unsettled by strange noises. Children will probably want an adult to sleep outside with them, which makes this a lovely family activity with the possibility of creating great memories.

➤ Make up beds on camp beds or inflatable mattresses. Alternatively, bring bed mattresses outside and place on a waterproof groundsheet to prevent moisture seeping in. Or sleep on raised areas, if available – for example, decking, veranda, balcony, terrace.

➤ Consider the alternative of using a bivouac sack (bivy bag) and sleeping mat to turn the night into a real survival adventure by sleeping further afield than the back garden; it's the kind of thing Enid Blyton's hardy Famous Five do in April (see *Five Get Into Trouble*). While I realise this may not appeal to all adults and children, for some a hike or walk over beautiful countryside, and a campfire or picnic supper followed by sleeping under the stars is the best way to enjoy the great outdoors.

➤ Sleeping wild for a night or two is permitted in many parts of the country, but check with the relevant authority/website before you set off.

Row, Row, Row a Boat

READING THE CLASSICS OF CHILDHOOD, you'd be forgiven for thinking our rivers and seas, lakes and ponds must be full of children (as well as Rat and Mole from Kenneth Grahame's *The Wind in the Willows*) sailing vessels of all kinds laden with maps, dogs, binoculars, tents, torches and plenty of food. According to fiction, our waterways are clogged with small craft taking their occupants on marvellous voyages of discovery to find treasure and adventure, or simply on wonderful, happy, fun-and-sandwich-filled days out.

I have visions of Enid Blyton's Famous Five in George's rowing boat hailing Rat and Mole in theirs, while the crews of the *Swallow* and the *Amazon* sail past with R.M. Ballantyne's Ralph, Jack and Peterkin following closely behind in their home-made *Coral Island* boat. Gerald Durrell in the *Bootle-Bumtrinket* is exploring the waters with his dog and collecting gear, while Tom Sawyer and Huckleberry Finn are whooping it up on their raft, looking for fast and dangerous water as the March sisters from Louisa May Alcott's *Little Women* – Meg, Jo, Beth and Amy – hug the river bank as they row their boat in a more quiet and sedate fashion (but Jo is secretly longing to leap on to Tom and Huck's raft). And little Jim Ruggles from *The Family from One End Street* by Eve Garnett is an inadvertent stowaway in a pipe on board a barge, and is having the adventure of a lifetime which will be retold with relish at the next meeting of the Gang of the Black Hand.

The great appeal of all these boats, rafts and coracles is that they are a marvellous form of transport and provide a temporary escape from the landlocked world – and rare is the child who isn't inspired to sail away into adventure or into the sunset.

 **PRACTICAL**

→ I am a great fan of the traditional boating lakes you find in municipal parks and at the seaside — the kind that still offer the chance to have some old-fashioned fun in shallow water. They make for timeless, simple Sunday afternoon outings with everyone twirling round and round in circles in their boats because no one can row properly.

→ Alternatively, you can sail and row in the same places as favourite writers and storybook characters:

→ Visit the Lake District and row a boat on Grasmere to see the world as Wordsworth saw it (or go to Ullswater where he rowed in a stolen boat as a young boy), or emulate the Swallows and Amazons on Coniston Water.

→ Hire boats in Famous Five country, near Corfe Castle, Dorset. Arrive by ferry, row up the River Frome from Wareham or sail from Swanage.

→ Look at www.gingerpop.co.uk for more ideas.

→ Hire a skiff on the Thames and travel from Kingston to Oxford like Jerome K. Jerome's *Three Men in a Boat*: www.riverthames.co.uk/boat/hire

→ Enjoy a fabulous view of Cambridge from a rowing boat or punt — or emulate Rupert Brooke and go further upriver to Grantchester and have a delicious afternoon tea at the Orchard Tea Garden www.orchard-grantchester.com.

MAKE-BELIEVE BOATS

For many children, it's the idea of being in a boat with all worldly possessions, a map and the prospect of imaginary adventure that appeals, and this means that pretend boats can be just as exciting as the real thing.

'Boats' can be built anywhere – indoors or out, on blankets, in boxes, on settees and chairs, on beds – and they are great for winter and wet-weather games.

Fly a Kite

DADS ARE BRILLIANT. But it's often the clever, quirky little things they can do rather than any grand gestures or paternal heroics that remain in the memory. Danny's dad in Roald Dahl's *Danny the Champion of the World* is exactly the kind of father that possesses all sorts of marvellous, useful and exciting skills.

"My father, without the slightest doubt, was the most marvellous and exciting father any boy ever had."

He's the dad of your dreams. He can mend cars, catch pheasants, make fire balloons, tree houses, bows and arrows, stilts, whizzers and boomerangs – and as he and Danny live a pretty bohemian life, the two of them can also be wonderfully spontaneous. If there's a wind, why not make a kite and fly it?

"'There's a good wind today,' he said one Saturday morning. 'Just right for flying a kite. Let's make a kite, Danny.'

So we made a kite."

Kite-making is one of those skills that are in danger of dying out. These days, there are fewer and fewer fathers, uncles and big brothers who know how to make a kite from a few pieces of wood, an old shirt and some string, and young boys (and girls) are missing out on the magic of flying a home-made kite. So watch carefully now as Danny's father demonstrates:

"He showed me how to splice four thin sticks together in the shape of a star, with two more sticks across the middle to brace it. Then we cut up an old blue shirt of his and stretched the material across the frame-work of the kite. We added a long tail made of thread, with little leftover pieces of the shirt

tied at intervals along it… and he showed me how to attach the string to the frame-work so that the kite would be properly balanced in flight."

Danny is amazed and thrilled that the kite flies successfully, rising up and bobbing for hours on the wind. Not every dad can make a kite, but every dad (or big brother/granddad/uncle) can have a go at flying one.

✑ PRACTICAL ✑

- There are plenty of books with good instructions for making kites, but various woodworking and manual skills are required, which may defeat some potential kite-makers. Also, and I do not want to dampen anyone's enthusiasm, there is nothing more disappointing than a kite made with high hopes that simply refuses to fly. So there is a good argument for buying a basic kite and learning how to fly it before attempting to make one. There is no use making everyone miserable by hammering and splicing and bracing, then finding the result won't get off the ground.

- There is just as much fun in taking a shop-bought kite and climbing a hill or going to a deserted park, field or beach on a blustery day, and watching your kite rise and bob and pull on the string. Young boys and girls will still think you are 'marvellous' for coming out and flying kites with them.

- Alternatively, the fun might be in making a kite to your own design, and messing about with sticks and shirts and string. As long as you remember to laugh if it (and your hopes) falls to earth with a crash. On the other hand, though, it may soar like Danny's.

Keep the Campfires Burning

MANY ADVENTURE BOOKS CONTAIN wonderful campfire scenes that are absolutely guaranteed to make the reader want to collect firewood, find a box of matches and a packet of marshmallows, and make a fire right now, this very minute. Who can resist the idea of huddling round a fire with friends, everyone wrapped in warm blankets, looking into the flames, drinking cocoa, telling stories and singing songs?

Many of the children who build them take great pride in making good, long-lasting fires. They know it's a valuable skill to acquire for keeping warm and dry on expeditions – and for rustling up sizzling sausages. The Swallows in *Swallows and Amazons* are particularly fussy about their campfires, and the author is keen that the reader should also build theirs correctly. This is how it is done:

"Mate Susan built a small fireplace of stones on the beach... The others gathered dry sticks that had been left all along the high-water mark. Susan took a few handfuls of dry leaves and moss. She put them in the middle of her fireplace and built a little wigwam over them with bits of dried reeds from last year... The she lit the moss and the reeds blazed up, while she built another wigwam over the reeds, this time of small sticks, all meeting at the middle over the blaze.

When they caught fire and began to crackle she piled bigger sticks against the small ones. In a few minutes she had a strong fire."

So now there's no excuse for a weak and smoky fire...

PRACTICAL

■→ Always check local bye-laws before building a fire. Many beaches and campsites prohibit fires.

THINGS TO DO ON OR AROUND A CAMPFIRE

■→ Boil a kettle of water and make mugs of steaming hot tea or cocoa.

■→ Toast sausages, bread, marshmallows.

■→ Bake potatoes in the embers (wrap in foil and nudge into the edge of the fire).

■→ Use old tins, for example, baked bean tins to cook food.

■→ Make campfire popcorn in parcels of tinfoil.

■→ Tell stories (ghost stories, 'dark and stormy night' stories, 'consequences' stories) and/or jokes.

■→ Sing songs. Now's your chance to bring out all the songs in your repertoire: repeating songs, action songs, folk songs, spirituals and rounds.

■→ Or just go into a campfire trance: look into the flames, listen to the sounds of a fire crackling and enjoy the simple, elemental pleasures of an outdoor fire.

This Little Piggy… Roast Pigs' Tails

I DON'T KNOW WHETHER TO LAUGH or recoil at the idea of roasting a pig's tail over a fire, but there's no doubt it intrigues me. I imagine many a child would be delighted to indulge in a little gory play before plunging a stick or skewer into the thick end of a pig's tail, holding it over a fire, and watching as the fat drips, bubbles and crackles over the flames and the skin turns dark and crispy. Then eating it.

You might be surprised to find that this treat comes from the apparently sweet and charming *Little House in the Big Woods* by Laura Ingalls Wilder. Except that beneath the book's sweetness and charm there is a story of difficult, often harsh, pioneering self-sufficiency, and many a battle with elements and enemies. And in this situation, should you be lucky enough to own or receive a pig, you make sure you eat all of it.

When Pa decides to kill the pig he's been fattening for winter, it's a huge family event. Pa saves the bladder and the tail for Laura and Mary; he makes a balloon out of the bladder (another ripping thing to do at butchering time) "but even better fun was the pig's tail". Pa skins it, pushes a sharp stick into the thick end and the girls take turns in holding it over coals.

"It sizzled and fried. And drops of fat dripped off and it blazed on the coals. Ma sprinkled it with salt. Their hands and faces got very hot… At last it was done. It was nicely browned all over, and how good it smelled! They carried it into the yard to cool it, and even before it was cool enough they began tasting it and burned their tongues. They ate every little bit of meat off the bones... and that was the end of the pig's tail. There would not be another one till next year."

Marvellous.

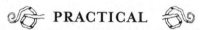 **PRACTICAL**

If you don't feel squeamish about handling pigs' tails (or bladders), roasting them in the simple and easy Little House-style over coals or a fire would be a brilliantly entertaining and memorable thing to do.

Winter Days

WHAT'S STRIKING ABOUT CHILDREN'S BOOKS set in winter is how much they form our perceptions of the season. Even as adults we carry around the images that have delighted us in stories, poems and fairy tales – images of crisp, pure air, a white, snow-filled landscape, icicles dangling from eaves and the shrieks of children sledging down hills, when unfortunately the reality in Britain is sadly much greyer and soggier. At a time when weather patterns are changing and the boundaries with autumn on one side and spring on the other have become less defined, it can be difficult to see winter as a separate, distinctive part of the year – unless you cosy up with a pile of good books such as *The Lion, the Witch and the Wardrobe, Winter Holiday, The Peppermint Pig* and the Little House books.

As young readers venture through the medium of words into a winter wonderland, they access all sorts of fabulous images and discover countless ways to make the most of this time of year – whether it's a mild winter or a full-on snowstorm. It may be that some of these are possible only in the imagination and from a comfy armchair or in a pretend arctic adventure, or it may be that there are opportunities to get outside and do it all for real. Whatever the situation, books have plenty of ripping things to do in winter. There's energetic fun with toboggans, skates, snowmen and snowballs, igloos and snow angels, there's dreamy contemplation of landscapes transformed overnight by a silent, magical snowfall, and there's plenty of toast and tea.

One thing's for sure. Once a child has experienced old-fashioned, snowy, icy winters in books, they will be quite certain that Nancy will be proved wrong when she says at the beginning of *Winter Holiday*, "You know what it's like. Dark at tea-time and sleeping indoors: nothing ever happens in the winter holidays."

Make Snow Pictures

THERE ARE SO MANY CHILDREN in books doing ripping things in the snow that, as it becomes increasingly rare – certainly in Britain – it must be difficult for modern children not to feel very wistful and just a little sad to be missing out on so much fun.

All the more reason then, for them to be ready with plenty of ideas for things to do when it does finally snow and they can throw themselves into enjoying it. Maybe literally, like Laura and Mary in *The Little House in the Big Woods* by Laura Ingalls Wilder, who, even though they know the snow is going to stick around for the whole winter, still run outside enthusiastically with their cousins on Christmas Eve to make "snow pictures".

"The way they did it was this:

Each one by herself climbed up on a stump, and then all at once, holding their arms out wide, they fell off the stumps into the soft, deep snow. They fell flat on their faces. Then they tried to get up without spoiling the marks they made when they fell. If they did it well, there in the snow were five holes, shaped almost exactly like four little girls and a boy, arms and legs and all. They called these their pictures."

I wonder how many children make a fervent wish for snow at Christmas after reading this?

NOTE: There's another, sweet variation on this theme; if a child fall backwards on the snow then moves their arms and legs up and down before getting up, they make a snow angel.

Make Paper Snowflakes

Making paper snowflakes is an activity that satisfies both creative types (because they are beautiful decorations) and scientific ones (who are intrigued by the amazing structures and patterns of the real thing). Use white, silver or coloured paper that can be decorated with glitter, tinfoil and/or sequins.

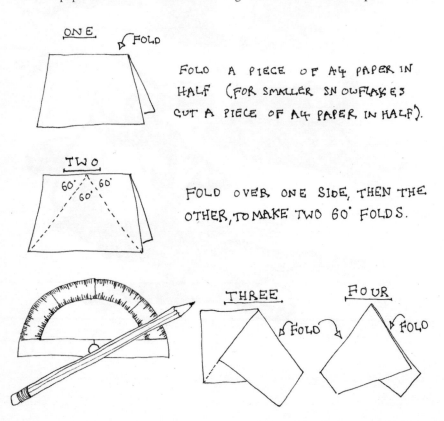

ONE

FOLD

FOLD A PIECE OF A4 PAPER IN HALF (FOR SMALLER SNOWFLAKES CUT A PIECE OF A4 PAPER, IN HALF).

TWO

60° 60°
60°

FOLD OVER ONE SIDE, THEN THE OTHER, TO MAKE TWO 60° FOLDS.

THREE

FOLD

FOUR

FOLD

FIVE

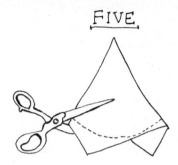

CUT OFF THE EDGES OF THE PAPER IN AN ARC, IF YOU WERE TO UNFOLD THE PAPER NOW (DON'T!) IT WOULD MAKE A CIRCLE.

SIX

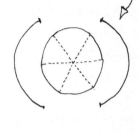

SEVEN

SNIP AWAY SMALL SECTIONS OF YOUR PAPER CAREFULLY WITH SCISSORS

EIGHT

UNFOLD THE PAPER CAREFULLY AND YOU WILL HAVE A
SNOWFLAKE

Recipe for a Perfect, Snowy, Winter's Day

IT'S VERY REFRESHING TO ENCOUNTER unreconstructed breakfast-eaters who relish a filling breakfast because they know they are going to use up every ounce of energy it provides. In *The Rat-a-Tat Mystery* by Enid Blyton the three children are excited by the prospect of a bright, snowy, winter's day just after Christmas. Their excitement is palpable and they eat an extra-smashing breakfast of porridge, bacon, eggs and toast to make sure they are well equipped calorie-wise for a morning's tobogganing.

It's one of my favourite winter scenes in literature. The children wrap up in scarves, gloves and thick sweaters (no doubt hand-knitted) and spend a magical day climbing up and down a hill fifty or sixty times before coming in for a deliciously warming vegetable stew. Then it's off out again for an afternoon of snowball fights and snow-house building, and finally some hot tea and more food before they close the curtains and collapse, tired but happy, into bed.

Fifty years on, this still sounds like a wonderful winter's day, so here is the recipe. If you can't find snow, ingredients such as fresh air, ball games, rolling down hills, walks in woods, making dens, roller-skating and cycling can be substituted.

✦ PRACTICAL ✦

Breakfast

- ✵ Creamy porridge
- ✵ Crispy bacon and fried eggs, and lots of toast (six slices if you are like Snubby)
- ✵ Followed by a morning's tobogganing

Lunch

- ✵ Lovely-smelling stew full of carrots and onions and turnips and parsnips
- ✵ A hot steamed pudding
- ✵ Followed by an epic snowball fight and igloo-building

A late tea

- ✵ Scalding hot tea from a big, brown teapot, plus poached eggs, toast and butter
- ✵ Followed by a good night's sleep

Make a Winter Holiday Hotpot

THE CHILDREN HAVE BEEN OUT ALL morning in the wonderland of a snow-covered Lake District. They've worked hard covering an old hut with snow to transform it into an igloo. And now it's time for lunch. So what's the very best thing to cook and eat in a hand-built igloo? Well, a steaming-hot hotpot, of course.

After a long, freezing day on the ice many a polar explorer would no doubt give his eye teeth to eat a plateful of the delicious hotpot the Swallows and Amazons prepare and enjoy in *Winter Holiday* in their perfectly domed, strangely cosy igloo. When the young adventurers come in for lunch they find that "Susan and Peggy had been making a hot-pot, with potatoes, onions and carrots, and a whole tin of bully beef" and clouds of steam are rising from the pot in the tradition of all good, home-made, unrushed hot-pots. But as the contents of the pot are too hot to eat immediately, it is transferred to the natural refrigerator of the icy outdoors to cool down. And then:

"... it was taken back into the igloo to be eaten. The explorers sat round it on benches and logs under the light of the lantern that was hanging from... the roof. They had not enough spoons and forks for everybody, but fingers, as Roger said, came in useful."

So fingers serve as cutlery and sandwiches as edible plates that also rather deliciously soak up juices in the process, and I imagine that at this point every young reader is wishing himself to the North Pole just so he can really and truly appreciate a good hotpot.

✂ PRACTICAL ✂

The great thing about hotpots is that they are simple, cheerful, cheap and expandable meals. They are a taste of childhood winters when your hands and toes and knees and nose are numb with cold, when you come in from playing outside or are preparing to make a bid for the North Pole after lunch. A hotpot is the ultimate one-pot meal that can be made by even the most inexperienced of cooks in the most basic conditions – even an igloo – as quantities do not have to be exact and can be stretched by the addition of extra vegetables. Lamb is the traditional meat in a hotpot made in the north-west England, and, as *Winter Holiday* is set in the Lake District, this is what the recipe calls for. It's a sort of Cumbrian tattie pot without the black pudding.

IGLOO HOTPOT

Serves 6–8

250 g per person boned shoulder of lamb, trimmed and cut into 2 cm cubes

1 large or 2 medium onions

2 garlic cloves, chopped (optional)

400 g organic carrots (6 or 7 carrots), cut into rounds approx 1 cm thick

900 g potatoes, peeled and sliced into rounds approx. 5 mm thick

3 tablespoons vegetable oil or mild olive oil, plus a little extra if needed

25 g butter (a large knob), plus extra for the potatoes

1 dessertspoon plain flour

75 cl–1 litre stock (home-made stock or stock made with liquid concentrate or a couple of stock cubes – vegetable, onion or beef stock is fine)

Salt and pepper

1. Preheat the oven to 150°C/Gas Mark 2.
2. Prepare the meat, onions, garlic (if using), carrots and potatoes as above. Keep the sliced potatoes in a pan of cold water until needed.
3. Put the oil in a large casserole or hotpot pot (one with a lid).
4. Brown the meat in the oil in two batches. Remove with a slotted spoon to a plate.
5. Add the butter to the oil (and add a little more oil, if necessary), tip in the onions, carrots, the garlic if you are using it, and cook gently with the lid on for 10 minutes to soften.
6. Scatter the flour over the vegetables, season with salt and pepper and cook for a couple of minutes.
7. Return the meat and its juices to the pan and stir well. Pour over enough stock to cover the contents. Simmer gently with the lid on for 10 minutes.
8. Remove the pan from the heat. Taste and adjust the seasoning if necessary. Arrange the slices of potatoes on top of the meat so that they overlap. Neat concentric circles are pleasing, but not vital to the success of the dish.
9. Cover with the lid and cook in the oven for 1 hour.
10. Now remove the lid, dot little dabs of butter on the surface and cook for a further 45–60 minutes. This is a forgiving dish that does not spoil with a little extra time in the oven.
11. To maintain hotpot tradition, serve with pickled red cabbage..

More Ripping, Snowy Things to Do.

➡ Keep a record of snowfall (over a winter, over time) by measuring the depth of the snow with a ruler.

➡ Look at snow under a microscope or magnifying glass to see the beautiful structure of snowflakes.

➡ See how clean or impure snow is by melting a small amount in a saucepan then boiling it until the water evaporates and leaves a residue

➡ Make ice and have ice experiments. When you know the temperature is going to fall below freezing overnight, make natural ice cubes or ice balls with unusual centres by leaving stones, leaves or dried flowerheads in bowls and ice-cube trays filled with water.

➡ Investigate bird, animal and shoe tracks in the snow.

➡ If you have plenty of snow, make an igloo or snow den.

➡ If you have plenty of ice, play a simple form of ice hockey with branches for sticks and stones for pucks. In Nina Bawden's *The Peppermint Pig*, the children play bandy on a huge ice slide using curved branches of willows for sticks.

➡ Go ice-skating. If you need a reason to do this, read the lovely scenes of skating on the Fens in *The Peppermint Pig* and Philippa Pearce's *Tom's Midnight Garden*. Although some people enjoy speed-skating and others go figure-skating, the vast majority skate purely for pleasure and to make the most of the ice. These days, there are so many temporary outdoor ice rinks that it's once again possible to experience the thrills and spills of skating outdoors in sparklingly cold fresh air.

Make a Toasting Fire

WHETHER YOU ARE A CHILD or an adult, there is nothing better on a cold evening than enveloping yourself in a long, woollen plaid dressing-gown tied with a silky, twisted cord, or a fluffy, brushed cotton version that boasts a good number of interesting buttons, and sitting round the fire toasting yourself. I also think it's a good idea to keep old and outgrown dressing-gowns available for visitors so that they can join in the fun of toasting themselves.

Mr Badger in *The Wind in the Willows* by Kenneth Grahame knows the value of dressing gowns. When Ratty and Mole appear out of the cold and snowy night after their adventure in the Wild Wood, he ushers the freezing and dispirited pair into his marvellously cosy, snug, well-stocked kitchen where he has been enjoying his supper.

"The kindly Badger thrust them down on a settle to toast themselves at the fire… then he fetched them dressing-gowns and slippers… [and] when at last they were thoroughly toasted, the Badger summoned them to the table, where he had been busy laying a repast." A little while later, "they gathered round the glowing embers of the great wood fire, and thought how jolly it was to be sitting up *so* late, and *so* independent, and *so* full."

This little scene sums up everything that is appealing to children about a night in front of a fire (ironically, it's somehow possible to stay up much later when you're dressed for bed). So turn down the heating, put on a dressing gown and, if it's possible, light a fire and toast both yourself and some food.

 **PRACTICAL**

Once children are old enough to be trusted with the operation, it's worth teaching them how to make a fire (or learning with them). There is nothing like the satisfaction of creating a long-lasting, flickering, crackling blaze. Plus, anyone who can light a fire will always be welcome in cold houses.

FOOD TO TOAST ON FIRES

Toasting food on a fire is one of the most exciting forms of cooking. Here are some suggestions for food to be toasted.

- In *Heidi* by Johanna Spyri, Heidi's grandfather toasts chunks of cheese until they begin to melt and then transfers them to slices of chewy, tasty bread.

- The children in *The Box of Delights* by John Masefield toast bread and dripping and sausages, lying on the hearth in front of a fire as part of their game of Robber Tea.

243

🌂 Milly-Molly-Mandy, little-friend-Susan and Billy Blunt enjoy fresh muffins (delivered by the Muffin-man) toasted on forks in the story 'Milly-Molly-Mandy Has Friends'.

🌂 Aunt Harriet makes toast on a brass fork and serves it with dripping, potato cakes, golden syrup and sticky caraway-seed biscuits in *The Peppermint Pig* by Nina Bawden.

🌂 Katie Morag and her cousins toast marshmallows on sticks on an outdoor fire in *Katie Morag and the Big Boy Cousins* by Mairi Hedderwick.

🌂 But the ultimate in food to cook over a fire has to be pigs' tails. This is what Laura and Mary do in *The Little House in the Big Woods* by Laura Ingalls Wilder. Oh yes, indeed. For more details turn to page 229.

10 books to read by the fire in winter

1. *Winter Holiday*, Arthur Ransome (snow and igloos)

2. **The Box of Delights, John Masefield (Christmas, New Year and posset)**

3. The Rat-a-Tat Mystery, Enid Blyton (snowy fun and mystery)

4. *Little Women*, (Christmas without presents)

5. **Ballet Shoes, Noel Streatfeild (Christmas with presents)**

6. The Little House books, Laura Ingalls Wilder (winter rituals and fun)

7. *The Peppermint Pig*, Nina Bawden (sliding and skating in the Fens)

8. **Five Go Adventuring Again, Enid Blyton (secrets and codes)**

9. A Little Princess, Frances Hodgson Burnett (cold, hungry heroine)

10. *The Mystery of the Secret Room*, Enid Blyton (Christmas holiday adventure)

Poems and Stories

UNSURPRISINGLY, BOOKS ARE A TREASURE trove of ripping things to do with words. Whether they are spoken, written, rhyming, simple, florid, printed or hand-written, words, poems, tales and stories can inspire a host of literary activities. One of the greatest benefits of reading from an early age is the development of a love of language, an ear for a beautiful sound, a taste for a delicious metaphor, an enriched vocabulary, a confidence with words, a vehicle for self-expression, and an ability to use words to amuse, to console, and to describe. Books inspire readers to build narratives, to write, to dabble, to play with words, and to try them out for size and fit.

The desire to tell stories is as old as man, and the words 'once upon a time' are the gateway to a different world. Small wonder, then, that huge numbers of children in books tell gripping stories to one another, like Katy in the loft in *What Katy Did* and Garnet and Citronella in their tree house in *Thimble Summer*. Some form their own storytelling clubs like the Gang of the Black Hand in *The Family from One End Street*, whose boy members try to outdo each other in tales of adventure (all borrowed from books and comics until John Ruggles has a real adventure, and even then the other boys don't believe him and accuse him of making it up or getting it out of a book). Then there are the story-writers like Dorothea in *Winter Holiday* who narrates her life to herself as she goes along, and others who have ambitions of becoming a writer – for example, Jo March in *Little Women*, who sits in her garret with her pet rat and a stash of apples, penning stories she hopes will one day be published (and the reader is as thrilled as she is when her hard work and determination pay off). There are even several budding playwrights and, in the character of William Brown, a playwright-actor-director.

There are also plenty of children who simply love words. Think of Anne of Green Gables and the way in which she memorises poems she doesn't fully understand because she simply adores the way they sound. Or Josie Smith who is captivated by the technical vocabulary on a packet of nasturtium seeds. Or Jennings and Darbishire in *Jennings Goes to School* who have great fun deciding on their fictional detective's name (the first name must have two syllables and the surname one – like Sherlock Holmes) and play with the sounds and syllables until they make a tongue-twister name no one can say.

The wonderful thing about books and stories and poems is that when all else fails and energy, imagination and inspiration are running low, their words have the power to restore the spirits, banish boredom and dispel disillusionment. All that's needed is just to curl up, snuggle up or stretch out on a hammock or on the floor and read or, like the Fossil sisters in *Ballet Shoes* on a wet day, listen to the wonderful words of the best children's writers.

Listen to a Story

ON WET DAYS "SYLVIA THOUGHT it was a good plan to stay in and make toffee or be read out loud to". What a great plan, but maybe an even better plan would be to stay in, listen to a story *and* make toffee. Because multitasking is one of the very best things about listening to a story, as the Fossil sisters, stars of the classic *Ballet Shoes* by Noel Streatfeild, know:

"Neither Pauline nor Petrova could sit quiet while they were being read to, however interesting the book, without something to do. Pauline had sewing, and embroidered very well for somebody not yet ten. Petrova was very stupid with a needle, but very neat with her fingers; she was working at a model made in Meccano. It was a difficult model of an aeroplane, meant for much older children to make."

As adults we know how enjoyable it is to doing something while listening to the radio or an audiobook, so it's difficult to understand why children are subjected to legs-crossed, sit-still, story times on carpets in school. Far better to make some toffee, get out *The Secret Garden* as the wise Sylvia does, and let children multitask. Even if the only other thing they are doing is lying on the floor, waving their legs and chewing happily.

PRACTICAL

- It's impossible to overstate the enormous value and shared pleasure of reading aloud to children from a very early age.
- Audiobooks are a good alternative, particularly for journeys, holidays

and days when a child is poorly.

🕷 It's bewildering that there are so few good radio programmes for children when it seems to be an ideal medium for them. There are a few, and it's worth searching the BBC radio website thoroughly for details (www.bbc.co.uk/radio). Then your children can be like the Ovaltineys, sitting around the radio in their dressing gowns with a nice hot drink and something good to listen to.

🕷 Activities that go well with listening to a story are: colouring in, tracing pictures, doodling, threading beads, knitting, sewing, jigsaws, sorting out/lining up/arranging cars and models and farm animals, dressing and undressing dolls and brushing their hair, making models, playing with bricks and construction sets. And eating toffee.

CHEWY TOFFEE

WARNING: It is extremely easy to make toffee is at home with excellent results. However, because of the dangers associated with the very high temperature of sugar, it should only ever be made by an adult while children watch at a sensible distance. Consider it a kind of kitchen spectator sport and do not attempt any tasting until the toffee is completely cold.

Makes I tray

Vegetable or mild olive oil, for greasing
340 g granulated sugar
225 g salted butter
200 g golden syrup

1. Oil a baking tray or tin approx. 20 × 26 cm with the vegetable oil or olive oil. You can use a different size tin if that's what you have. A smaller tin will give thicker toffee and a larger tin will give thinner toffee.
2. Place all the ingredients in a large saucepan with a heavy base.
3. Melt the ingredients *slowly* over a very low heat, stirring or shaking gently very occasionally. Allow up to 10 minutes for this.
4. Once everything has melted and the sugar has dissolved, bring the mixture slowly to the boil. While this is happening, fill a small cup or bowl with very cold water (add an ice cube or two in warm weather) and keep it to hand for testing the toffee.
5. After 6 minutes, drop a small amount of the toffee mixture into the cold water. If it hardens immediately but is still pliable, it is done. If not, carry on boiling and test every 30 seconds. Alternatively, if you are using a sugar thermometer boil until the liquid reaches 130°C and test. If the temperature goes higher than 130°C the toffee becomes less chewy and more brittle.
6. When the toffee is ready, remove the pan from the heat and pour the toffee mixture into the tin.
7. Leave to cool for 10–15 minutes then mark into squares with a sharp knife.
8. Allow the toffee to cool completely before removing it from the tin and cutting or breaking it into pieces.

Learn Poems by Heart

"DON'T YOU JUST LOVE POETRY THAT gives you a crinkly feeling up and down your back?" Anne of Green Gables asks the plain-living, unimaginative but very kind Marilla and, in the process, reminds us all of the pure, often physical, pleasure of poetry.

Like many children, Anne adores words. She scoops them up and stores them in her personal cache where they bide their time until they come rushing and gushing out of her, amusing and bemusing those around her. She even adores the sound of words she doesn't understand; as she says of one grandiose poem, "I don't know what 'squadrons' means nor 'Midian', either, but it sounds *so* tragical."

Anne wallows in the luxuriance of poetry, its glorious vocabulary, patterns, rhythms and sounds. She chooses works by German and Scottish Romantic poets to learn by heart, and immerses herself in their romance, tragedy and melodrama, their celebrations of nature and heroic deeds. She commits her favourite poems to memory so that she can always find solace and excitement in their overwrought language and emotions. She shows that children are quite capable of relishing grandiose, flamboyant language and can listen to, read, memorise and recite poems.

Discovering and declaiming poetry is a highly enjoyable thing to do at home. In fact, home is the ideal place for poetry; children are relaxed and receptive, and their anti-poetry barriers are down. So get out the poetry books, laugh at limericks, play with puns, imagine images and enjoy yourselves. That "crinkly feeling" is one worth experiencing.

Poetry, please:

1. Tyger! tyger! Burning bright

2. The Owl and the Pussy-Cat went to sea

3. *'You are old, Father William,' the young man said*

4. She walks in beauty, like the night

5. *In Xanadu did Kubla Khan*

6. I met a traveller from an antique land

7. How do I love thee? Let me count the ways.

8. *Season of mists and mellow fruitfulness*

9. If you can keep your head when all about you

10. *Faster than fairies, faster than witches*

* First lines from: 1. 'The Tyger' by William Blake, 2. 'The Owl and the Pussy-Cat' by Edward Lear, 3. 'Father William' by Lewis Carroll, 4. 'She Walks in Beauty' by Lord Byron, 5. 'Kubla Khan' by Samuel Taylor Coleridge, 6. 'Ozymandias of Egypt' by Percy Bysshe Shelley, 7. 'How Do I Love Thee?' by Elizabeth Barrett Browning, 8. 'To Autumn' by John Keats, 9. 'If' by Rudyard Kipling, 10. 'From a Railway Carriage' by Robert Louis Stevenson

Poets whose work is particularly suitable for children
* Spike Milligan
* Robert Louis Stevenson, especially *A Child's Garden of Verses*
* Roger McGough
* Charles Causley
* Michael Rosen
* A.A. Milne
* Edward Lear
* Walter de la Mare
* Lewis Carroll
* Rudyard Kipling

Poets whose work gives the "crinkly feeling"
* Shakespeare
* Edward Thomas
* Alfred, Lord Byron
* W.B. Yeats
* William Wordsworth
* Wilfred Owen
* John Keats
* Robert Frost
* Elizabeth Barrett Browning
* Gerard Manley Hopkins

Excellent anthologies
* *Read Me* and *Read Me 2* (Macmillan)
* *The Works* and *The Works 2* (Macmillan)
* *The Rattle Bag* ed. Seamus Heaney and Ted Hughes (Faber, 2005)
and *By Heart* ed. Ted Hughes (Faber, 2002)

Enjoy a Dark and Stormy Night

HACKNEYED? CERTAINLY. A cliché? Oh, yes. But there aren't many opening lines that create such a thrill, such a sense of excitement and anticipation, as 'It was a dark and stormy night'.

There is no better way to enjoy wild weather, tossing trees, lashing rain, howling winds, dark clouds and moon shadows than wrapped up in a comfy dressing gown while sitting on a bed or by a window (think of *The Sound of Music* and all that lovely nightwear when the children pile into Maria's room during a violent storm). Then, when the storm abates or you have been sufficiently entertained or perhaps terrified by the spectacle, you can go downstairs to a bright and cosy kitchen and have an impromptu midnight supper with the other sleepless people in your house.

This ripping thing to do is inspired by the wonderfully evocative opening scene in *A Wrinkle in Time* by Madeleine L'Engle (first line: 'It was a dark and stormy night') when Meg Murry is unable to sleep through the storm in her shivery-cold attic bedroom.

"– I'll make myself some cocoa, she decided. – That'll cheer me up."

As soon as she reaches the kitchen, she finds a lovely contrast to what's going on outside; her brother is calmly drinking milk and eating bread and jam while the dog is lying happily under the table. Their mother joins them and cocoa and sandwiches are made: "liverwurst-and cream-cheese" for Mrs Murry, tomato for Meg.

"Meg knelt at her mother's feet. The warmth and light of the kitchen had relaxed her so that her attic fears had gone. The cocoa steamed fragrantly in the saucepan; geraniums bloomed on the windowsills and there was a bouquet of tiny yellow chrysanthemums in the center of the table. The curtains, red, with a blue and green geometrical pattern, were drawn, and seemed to reflect their cheerfulness throughout the room."

Order is apparently restored...

WHAT YOU NEED

- A dark and stormy night when no one can sleep
- A warm, bright kitchen
- A dog or cat (optional)
- Cheerful flowers in pots or vases
- Dress code: nighties, pyjamas, warm socks, slippers and dressing gowns

WHAT TO DO

- Batten down the hatches, close the windows and curtains, make the kitchen cosy and warm.
- Prepare cocoa, hot milk, toast and butter, bread and jam, sandwiches with unusual combinations of fillings (midnight suppers provide the perfect moment to experiment).
- Talk, play cards, listen to descriptions and news of the storm on local radio.
- Read aloud: *A Wrinkle in Time* for older readers, or *It Was a Dark and Stormy Night* by Janet and Allan Ahlberg (Puffin, 1998) for younger ones. Both live up to the promise of the first line.
- Or simply take it in turns to tell a story. Begin with the line, 'It was a dark and stormy night...'

A Few Marvellous Memoirs

SOMETIMES IT'S GOOD TO FIND out what sorts of ripping things real children did once upon a time, and this is when we should to turn to the classic memoirs of childhood. In some ways, the best of these are like the great classics of children's fiction in that they open up a new and different world to readers, introduce them to intriguing, often hilariously eccentric, casts of characters and show them the process of growing-up from someone else's perspective.

Memoirs can be enjoyed by older readers (eleven plus) and adults alike, and are variously inspirational, endearing, revealing, hysterically funny, affectionate and poignant, vivid and evocative, and full of details of what real children once did. The best contain an elegiac, wistful and gently nostalgic quality but are never cloying or self-pitying, and they are stuffed with great ideas for things to do. The following are highly recommended:

Country childhoods

* *Cider with Rosie*, Laurie Lee
* *Lark Rise to Candleford*, Flora Thompson
* *The Country Child*, Alison Uttley

Eccentric families

* *Hons and Rebels*, Jessica Mitford
* *Period Piece*, Gwen Raverat
* *My Family and Other Animals*, Gerald Durrell

Growing up in America

* *The Life and Times of the Thunderbolt Kid*, Bill Bryson
* *My Life and Hard Times*, James Thurber

Dear Diary...

YOU ONLY HAVE TO WANDER through stationery stores and departments with their vast displays of diaries to know that diary-writing is not yet a lost art. They lure the would-be diarist with all those beautiful, empty pages waiting to be filled up with secrets, dreams, wishes, longings, birthdays, anniversaries, lists, resolutions and, if you're a teenager, thousands of exclamation points and smiley faces!!!!! ☺☺☺

Despite the fact that many forms of communication are now electronic, paperless and high-tech, young readers are still lapping up books written as diaries that inspire them to write their own. Whether it's classic (and real-life) diaries such as Anne Frank's or more contemporary (fictional) ones such as Adrian Mole's diaries by Sue Townsend, *Secrets* by Jacqueline Wilson and Meg Cabot's Princess Diaries series, they all help the reader to see there's nothing like telling your own story in your own voice in a private, personal place, away from prying eyes. Keeping a diary is also an excellent way of developing writing skills – and remember, many a famous writer's earliest efforts are to be found in youthful diaries.

PRACTICAL

 Choose a diary that suits a child's age; large, page-a-day desk diaries are more suited to verbose, fast-writing teenagers, while younger children like smaller diaries or diaries that tie in with favourite writers (Eric Carle, Jacqueline Wilson). If privacy is needed, buy a diary with a lock;

and if the writer wants to be able to look back at him/herself and him/her life over a period of time, invest in a five-year diary.

☂ A diary need not demand a lifetime or even a year's commitment. Summer diaries or holiday diaries can be fun and creative. With a scrapbook format, the diarist can add souvenirs (sugar sachets, tickets, receipts, photos, dried flowers) and drawings and sketches. Children may enjoy doing this together or on their own.

☂ Inspirational diarists are Virginia Woolf, Samuel Pepys, Vera Brittain, Captain Scott and Charles Darwin.

Growing Up

FROM THE AGE OF EIGHT OR SO, around the time that they start to become independent and fluent readers, it's clear that children are very definitely beginning to grow up, to have a sense of self and a desire to demonstrate that they are no longer 'little', but are independent and capable of doing much more grown-up stuff. Such as owning a penknife and using it sensibly like Nicola in *Autumn Term*, or earning money like the children in *Linnets and Valerians*, or directing a hedge post office like the March girls and Laurie in *Little Women*, or restoring the fortunes of the family like the Bastables in *The Story of the Treasure-Seekers*, or feeling entitled, like Betsy and Tacy, to a little more privacy and the personal, private space of a wooden piano box.

This is a time when books can be of immense value in offering both inspiration and reassurance. Many great stories for children in the eight- to twelve-year range chart the ups and downs, the frustrations and rewards of the rites of passage. They often feature children who are just a little older than their target readers, but this is why they are so useful: children are always ready to read about children who are a little further along the path to adulthood, who can show them the pitfalls, and the difficulties, and suggest ways of dealing with new challenges and new situations. These characters are reliable role models and the situations they deal with offer solutions to the problems of growing up. How do you get someone to write a letter to you? How do you write a newspaper? How do you find your own space in a busy household? How can you earn money? And how can you convince your parents you're old enough to have a penknife? Children will find all the answers they need in books.

Earn Money

MONEY IS A BURNING ISSUE WITH children in books (and real life for that matter); they need an unlimited supply in order to fund their extravagant ice creams and comic-reading lifestyles. They also need to learn how to make it — the sooner, the better, some parents might say. But what are the best ways of earning money when a child is too young to go out to work and chimney sweeps are no longer required?

Well, there are some excellent literary role models in books. Take, for example, the four orphaned Linnet children in Elizabeth Goudge's enchanting *Linnets and Valerians.* When they descend unexpectedly on their Uncle Ambrose one summer, he is quick to make sure the arrangement will profit all parties, and draws up a list of jobs that can be done in return for pocket money.

"6d for a barrowful of weeds

6d/week for grooming the horse and polishing his harness

6d/week for darning socks

1d/week for helping with the washing-up

6d/week for cleaning shoes

3d for a bucketful of snails"

Although some of the tasks and rates are outdated, Uncle Ambrose's down-to-earth, non-negotiable approach is very sensible. In modern parlance, it's a win–win situation and he's evidently a canny managing director in the boardroom of domestic business.

And the payback? Well, it comes with interest. Uncle Ambrose creates such a purposeful yet relaxed framework for living in harmony that the outcome is excellent. The children have a marvellous time, he has darned socks and a weed-free garden, and they all have "a wonderful summer, with one happy thing after another falling into place like pearls threaded on a string".

Now that's something worth earning.

IDEAS FOR MAKING MONEY

- Read *The Story of the Treasure Seekers* by E. Nesbit for all sorts of interesting and madcap money-making ideas. The Bastable children sell poetry, gossip, newspapers, sherry and even their own disgusting patent medicine. They also dig for treasure and are so desperate at one point that they take Albert-next-door hostage and demand a ransom.

- Go on the stage and earn money from performing like the characters in Noel Streatfeild's *Ballet Shoes* and *Dancing Shoes*. Or sell tickets to a home or garden performance featuring local talent. Or put on a circus and charge for entry.

- Go mushrooming and sell the mushrooms to a greengrocer as Kate does to pay for her new school hat in *The Family from One End Street* by Eve Garnett.

- Seek or dig for hidden/buried treasure. There are plenty of inspirational books on this theme: *Treasure Island* by Robert Louis Stevenson, *The Treasure Hunters* and the Famous Five series by Enid Blyton, *The Minnow on the Say* by Philippa Pearce.

- Or use Milly-Molly-Mandy's enterprising investment scheme in 'Milly-Molly-Mandy Spends a Penny' by Joyce Lankester Brisley. In this story she is able to spend a penny over and over again by being patient and doing things in a sound financial order. She finds a penny, asks advice from her family as to what she should do with it and is given six different ideas – all of which she wants to do. So she buys a packet of mustard and cress which she grows and then sells to Mrs Moggs at a profit. Next she buys a skein of rainbow wool and knits a kettle-holder for Mother who pays her for it. Next she invests in a patty pan and bakes cakes in it, one of which is sold to a passing lady cyclist, and Mother gives her 1d to cover the cost. Then she buys aniseed balls, and as she still has 1d left Grandpa puts it in the bank for her. All she has to do is save 3d more to be able to achieve her ambition to buy her own duckling. In such ways are entrepreneurs created and business empires built.

HOW NOT TO DO IT

Richmal Crompton's William stories are a fund of hilarious, misguided attempts to make money, such as selling Ginger's twin brothers ('William Sells the Twins' in *William Again*) and organising a dire 'Collection of Insects' to show to the paying public ('William the Showman' in *William – the Fourth*) as well as various shows and performances that invariably misfire.

Create a Newspaper

SOMETIMES THE ONLY WAY TO GET your name in a headline is to put it there yourself and there are some wonderful examples of enterprising young newspaper men and women in children's books who revel in the power of the press. *The Sunday Visitor*, written and edited single-handedly by Katy in Susan Coolidge's *What Katy Did* is perhaps the example to avoid. More democratic is *The Pickwick Portfolio*, the newspaper written with astonishing professionalism by Meg, Jo, Beth and Amy in *Little Women* by Louisa May Alcott. But my own subscription would have to go to *The Lewisham Recorder*, written and illustrated at the nursery table by the Bastable children in E. Nesbit's *The Story of the Treasure Seekers*. Like many a hardened hack before and since, they make no bones about writing with a view to commercial success.

"Every paper is written for some reason. Ours is because we want to sell it and get money. If what we have written brings happiness to any sad heart we shall not have laboured in vain. But we want the money too."

The children write a newspaper full of the things they find interesting: a consequences-style all-in-one serial (each part is written by a different person), dreadful poetry, random advice, useless information and plenty of childish non sequiturs. Albert-next-door's generous uncle has this unintentionally funny masterpiece typeset and the children send copies to all their friends, then realise there's no one left to buy it. So their money-making scheme comes to nought apart from two shillings from the uncle, and "you can't restore fallen fortunes on two shillings!"

PRACTICAL

The beauty of making your own newspaper is the mix of simplicity (just do it) and possibility (no deadlines, no style guides, no publication schedule, no set format). Paper and pens and plenty of ideas are all that's required. The articles can be written out by hand and collated but, and this is one thing I will say in favour of computers, you can also produce amazingly impressive effects with simple desk-top publishing (children are remarkably creative with page layouts, fonts, colours and illustrations).

As for content, well I think there's plenty in the Bastable newspaper that still appeals: stories, news, announcements, letters and miscellaneous advice. But there's more that can be included, such as:

- Family news
- Meal and food reviews
- Sports stories
- Fashion articles
- Travel and holiday pages
- School events
- Book, film, music reviews
- Pet stories
- Horoscopes
- Cutting-edge interviews
- Photos and illustrations

Run Your Own Post Office

IS IT ANY WONDER IN THESE DAYS OF RAPID, paperless, faceless, electronic communications that many children are still entranced by the idea of receiving old-fashioned letters in old-fashioned envelopes through the old-fashioned letter box? My children are not above sending off for free samples just for the thrill of getting something addressed to them through the post, and even their bank statements are opened with glee. When she was younger, Alice created her own little letter box from a shoe box, and for quite some time her dad and I had to drop in a note or letter or card after she had gone to bed so that she had something to open in the morning. It wasn't difficult – more a matter of simply remembering, finding variations on our stationery and thinking up little messages – but it was incredibly important to Alice.

This is why I think that many children would love to run their own little post office, something like the P.O. set up by Laurie and the March girls in Louisa May Alcott's *Little Women*, in an old bird box in the hedge that runs between their two houses. It's big enough to hold "letters, manuscripts, books, and bundles" and each party has a key to the box. But it's the imaginative way in which it is used that makes it so appealing and such a great inspiration:

"The P.O. was a capital little institution, and flourished wonderfully, for nearly as many queer things passed through it as through the real office. Tragedies and cravats, poetry and pickles, garden-seeds and long letters, music and ginger-bread, rubbers, invitations, scoldings and puppies. The old gentleman [Laurie's grandfather] liked the fun, and amused himself by sending odd bundles, mysterious messages, and funny telegrams." In a foreshadowing of future uses and events, his gardener even sends a love letter to Hannah, the housekeeper, c/o Jo.

How could anyone give up on real mail after reading that?

PRACTICAL

Setting up a home post office is very straightforward, but it also has plenty of scope for development; once the participants are involved, they will no doubt come up with plenty of good ideas of their own.

SETTING UP A POST OFFICE

- ➡ A post office can be created anywhere in the house, flat or garden – a hedge is not essential. Use an old shoe box, or a larger box of you intend to post bigger items. Cut a rectangular hole, paint or spray-paint the box or cover it with coloured paper, and write on collections times etc. If you plan to leave the post box outside it needs to be weather-, bird- and squirrel-proof, with a lid that lifts and shuts tightly.

- ➡ There are a couple of commercial toy post office sets which are good for getting started. The Postman Pat brand has a great refill pack of stamps and forms, and the Casdon Toy Post Office is excellent.

- ➡ On the other hand, it's very cheap and easy to make all you need from scratch, especially now that all types of documents and templates can be printed off computers. Older children can design their own documents, too.

- ➡ Design and make postage stamps on paper or light card, or use stickers. Used stamps may come in handy (you'll need paper glue to restick them).

➤ Buy date stamps and ink pads at stationery shops (we use Ryman www.ryman.co.uk) or look in craft shops such as Hobbycraft (www.hobbycraft.co.uk) for a wider range of stamps.

➤ Collect brown paper, string, rubber bands, sticky labels, Sellotape for parcels. Reuse large and padded envelopes.

➤ Use kitchen scales for weighing letters and parcels, and a calculator for working out prices. Create postcards with photos or with images downloaded from the computer and printed on light card. Recycle old cards, cut out pictures and illustrations and use them to make 'collage' cards (see page 58).

➤ Use plastic pretend money, Monopoly money or set up your own bank and design and issue paper notes and coins. Or collect small change and foreign coins and 'bag it up'.

➤ Visit a real post office for inspiration.

Write a Letter

IT MAY BE DIFFICULT FOR ADULTS TO PERSUADE modern children that the art of letter-writing is one worth acquiring, but the young letter writers of literature put forward plenty of good reasons.

To ask a huge favour. In E. Nesbit's *The Railway Children*, the polite begging the children send to the top-hatted gentleman on the train brings a hamper full of expensive food for their invalid mother, and a wonderful person into their lives.

To earn money. Noel Bastable in *The Story of the Treasure Seekers* by E. Nesbit writes a brief, unapologetic letter to a newspaper editor asking him to publish his poetry: "Dear Mr Editor, I want you to print my poetry and pay for it." You have to admire his direct style; at least you know where you stand with this poet.

To keep a family together in difficult times. In Louisa May Alcott's *Little Women* Meg, Jo, Beth and Amy write letters to Marmee who is away in Washington nursing their sick father. It's hard not to envy Mrs March receiving "plump envelopes" filled with such intensely individual missives from each of her daughters.

To solve mysteries and to practise different hand-writing styles. As practised by Fatty and the rest of the Five Find-Outers in Enid Blyton's *The Mystery of the Spiteful Letters.*

To summon help when trapped (and a chance to use invisible ink). Fatty, again, uses his letter-writing skills and invisible ink to let the others know his predicament when he finds himself in a locked room in *The Mystery of the Secret Room.*

In return for an excellent education. Jean Webster's *Daddy-Long-Legs* must have inspired generations of readers to write letters. Judy Abbott is sent to college by an anonymous benefactor ('Daddy-Long-Legs') and all she has to do in return is write to him every month. A richly rewarding relationship is forged,

the nature of the letters changes over time and if I say any more I'll be giving away too much. Read it.

To share secrets. Tom in Philippa Pearce's *Tom's Midnight Garden* writes 'reports' of the strange and wonderful garden goings-on to his brother at home because he knows no one else will believe him and, if they do find out, they'll put a stop to the magical adventures.

To alleviate loneliness and make exciting discoveries in the process. It is when the bored, unhappy and lonely Tom in Betsy Byar's *The Midnight Fox* seeks a quiet place to write a letter to his best friend Petie that he first catches sight of the black fox that changes his summer and his life for ever.

To keep parents and teachers happy. In Anthony Buckeridge's Jennings books, Jennings and Darbishire have to write weekly letters home from boarding school and their efforts are funny, revealing and incredibly badly written. But they prove that any letter is better than no letter.

But the best reason of all is the simple, unalloyed pleasure of receiving letters in return. Milly-Molly-Mandy articulates every child's wishful thinking in Joyce Lankester Brisley's 'Milly-Molly-Mandy Writes Letters' when the postman knocks on the door and she runs "hop-skip down to passage to look in the letter-box because she always sort of hoped there might be a letter for her!"

But there wasn't.

"I do wish the postman would bring me a letter sometimes... He never does."

Her ever-practical mother offers some sound advice:

"If you want the postman to bring you letters you'll have to write them to other people first."

The problem is knowing who to write to, but fortunately Aunty has two nieces and a nephew in America, and Milly-Molly-Mandy happily writes a chatty letter on fancy notepaper. After a long, long wait she finally receives *three* letters – and confirmation that you need to write a letter to get a letter.

HOW TO GET STARTED

- Buy nice paper and envelopes, or decorate plain paper with stickers and drawings. Mini-envelopes are particularly appealing; www.ideal-envelopes.co.uk has a fantastic range.

- Illustrate letters, like famous letter writers such as Beatrix Potter, Edward Lear and Lewis Carroll who drew exquisite and amusing illustrations in their letters.

- Enclose something tiny and/or light such as a pressed flower, a sheet of stickers, a photo, a drawing, a few used stamps for collections, a local postcard, a small sweet or stick of chewing gum, a little envelope of seeds from the garden, a chain of paper dolls (see page 53) or a funny or pretty collage (see page 58).

- Go to the post office to buy nice stamps – ask to see recent issues or stock up on particularly attractive or interesting ones when they come out.

- Find a pen friend. It's good to know there are still post-only pen-friend organisations such as International Pen Friends www.penfriends.org; look on the internet for further details.

Private Spaces

WHAT IS IT ABOUT BIG BOXES THAT is irresistible to children? Ever since they were tiny, all three of my children have been drawn more to the packaging than to the contents of boxes. And this makes me wish I'd had a copy of *Betsy-Tacy* by Maud Hart Lovelace to hand when they were growing up, so that we could have talked about what is probably the ultimate in play boxes, Betsy and Tacy's wooden piano box (and I could have been reassured to discover that I wasn't the only mother ever to encourage eccentric box behaviour).

"This was their headquarters, their playhouse, the center of all their games. It stood behind Betsy's house... it was tall enough to hold a piano; so of course it was tall enough to hold Betsy and Tacy... this was Betsy's and Tacy's private corner. Betsy's mother was a great believer in people having private corners."

The two little girls make their wooden box cosy and comfortable by decorating the walls with magazine pictures, importing a rug and makeshift furniture, and keeping their treasures ("stones and moss") in a shoe box (another lovely use of a box). It's a special space, rather like a box in the theatre, from which Betsy and Tacy can see and be seen, and it can also be a millinery store, a lemonade store and a sand store. In fact, it can be anything they want it to be and that, I think, is the lure of the big box.

Children don't need much to fire their imaginations; an expensive playhouse is all well and good, but they often prefer something a little less planned. I am sure they sense that a pretty pre-fab house comes with a catch — the expectation that they should play in it the way that the adults who design and like it think it ought to be used. By comparison, a large, sturdy empty box

offers much more scope for the imagination; once it is emptied of its contents, its purpose is also removed and it can be transformed into something quite different. It may be a house or a shop or a hospital or a spacecraft or a den or a bubble or a caravan or castle – the list of possibilities is endless.

As a box-deprived child, I would have loved a wooden piano box of my own. But a big cardboard box would have come a close second.

❧ PRACTICAL ☙

- Don't automatically throw away large delivery boxes and don't assume a child is too old to want to play in one. Even teenagers enjoy cutting windows, spray-painting graffiti or decorations on the walls, both inside and out (it's good to encourage their Banksy tendencies), and crawling into a cardboard den with a blanket and a book or a friend.
- There are some excellent cardboard structures on the market. They can

be used indoors or taken outdoors in fine weather, and can be folded away when not in use. The best range comes from Ecocentric (www.ecocentric.co.uk). We tested their 'pod', which is sturdy and large enough to hold two teenagers (at a nice, comfortable squeeze) and therefore fine for smaller children, and is sufficiently underdesigned to allow for full roaming of the imagination. If you want something with a little more purpose, this company also offers a cardboard igloo, a teepee, a den and a rocket.

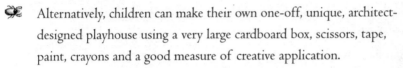 Alternatively, children can make their own one-off, unique, architect-designed playhouse using a very large cardboard box, scissors, tape, paint, crayons and a good measure of creative application.

Be Prepared: Penknives

Twentieth-century literature is full of self-reliant, capable children who carry penknives in their pockets. In this, they resemble the many thousands of children who were reading the books at the time they were published. For all these children, fictional or real, it would have been unthinkable to leave the house without their trusty penknife, because this would mean they weren't prepared for adventure.

So Richmal Crompton's William is delighted to find a new penknife amongst his Christmas gifts, and Jack in Enid Blyton's *The Secret of Spiggy Holes* would be lost without his. Billy Blunt fishes his out of a pocket to slice onions when he's at Milly-Molly-Mandy's house, and in *Coral Island* by R.M. Ballantyne, when Ralph, Jack and Peterkin are newly shipwrecked and turn out their pockets they are relieved to find they at least have a broken penknife.

But the best, shiniest, and most impressive penknife belongs to a girl. In *Autumn Term* by Antonia Forest Nicola and her twin Lawrie are allowed to choose a parting present from their parents when they go to boarding school. Lawries goes for a watch, but Nicola "plumped for the knife with sixteen blades which had dazzled her for months every time she passed the ironmonger's window where it was the centre-piece".

On the train to school, she shows it off proudly to a new friend: "Look. Sixteen blades *and* a corkscrew *and* a file *and* a thing for taking things out of horses' hooves." But at that very moment they swing round a bend and the penknife falls out of the open window. So Nicola does what any self-respecting penknife owner would do and pulls the communication cord. The guard is not amused.

Talk to any adult who owned a penknife when they were younger, and start waxing lyrical about the multitude of uses to which it, allegedly, could be put (no matter that no one ever used the tool for taking stones out of horses' hooves — it was *essential*), the feel of it in the pocket, the way it made them feel accomplished and ready for any practical challenge. They recall how getting their penknife was a rite of passage, an acknowledgement by grown-ups that you could be trusted not to hack your fingers off.

Things haven't changed so much. There are still plenty of young 'uns who are proud of their penknives and who see them as marvellous, multifunctional tools and not weapons. And what else would they use for the timeless, time-wasting but very satisfying activity of whittling sticks?

PRACTICAL

- Always defer giving a penknife to a child until you are happy he/she can use it with confidence.
- A good-quality penknife with fewer applications is better and safer than a cheaper one with a multitude of useless tools.
- Victorinox Swiss Army knives are still the best bet for younger users.
- For older children, look at the range of brilliantly designed Leatherman penknives.
- Be prepared for a few minor cuts. Show them where to find the plasters because they will be too embarrassed to ask.
- Knives with a locking device (any lock knives) are illegal. Many of them look like penknives but beware — they could get your child into huge trouble with the police. If in doubt, seek advice from a reputable retailer.

Treats and Remedies

EVERY CHILD, NO MATTER HOW BRAVE and bold, confident and independent, needs to be made to feel special; and every child needs comfort and consolation, reassurance and cheering up, plus plenty of little treats to reward and boost confidence and to right wrongs.

Being a child is hard work, so it's inevitable there will be off-days and poorly days and grumpy days when parents and carers need ideas to soothe, amuse and perk up jaded spirits. Sometimes a big hug and a little looking after are all that's needed when the world seems too big and brutish, or your head hurts and your throat is burning, and you want someone to feel very sorry for you. And sometimes something a little more creative and inventive may be needed to do the trick.

A get-better box of the type made by kind Mrs Cocoa Jones to amuse the tired, cross and spotty Naughty Little Sister is a great stand-by when children are stuck in bed. Breakfast in bed, complete with a squirty grapefruit, as enjoyed by Paddington Bear, is a lovely treat when ill, or indeed at any time. There are also plenty of ideas for treats and remedies in the stories of some of literature's most famous child invalids; Katy in *What Katy Did* writes Valentine verses, Pollyanna plays the "glad game" and Colin in *The Secret Garden* is cheered immensely by some very welcome if unorthodox visitors in the shape of Dickon and his animal friends.

And what sort of treats do non-poorly children enjoy? Well, it's noticeable that they are rarely expensive and/or made of plastic. In fact, the great thing about the treats described in books is that they are usually very simple and inexpensive, and rely more on gifts of time and thoughtfulness. Just being with grown-ups is often a treat; think of Laura and Mary's pleasure (and all the useful things they learn) when they are allowed to help their parents in the Little House books, or Josie Smith's delight when her harassed, busy mother finds time to dye Easter eggs with her. Others are treated to the type of personalised, home-made treats that children adore, like the carefully wrapped and labelled tray of food Chunky's mother prepares for him to eat when she is out in *The Adventures of Chunky*, or the dainty little bedtime biscuits made by Marmaduke Scarlet for Maria in *The Little White Horse*. And there is not one child in literature who does not love a fuss on his or her birthday, and a spectacular birthday cake to mark the occasion.

Master the Art of Breakfast in Bed

NOW THIS MAY SOUND INDULGENT, but I think everyone should be allowed the wizard, ripping, supersmashing treat of eating breakfast in bed from time to time. I don't think the occasional room service is going to weaken morals or engender permanently lax attitudes to getting up, and I certainly don't think it should be only available to invalids. And anyway, everyone needs to master the art of eating breakfast in bed at some time in their life.

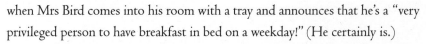

This is not as straightforward as you may think, as Paddington Bear discovers when Mrs Bird comes into his room with a tray and announces that he's a "very privileged person to have breakfast in bed on a weekday!" (He certainly is.)

"It was the first time he had ever had breakfast in bed and he soon found it wasn't as easy as it looked. First of all he had trouble with the grapefruit. Every time he pressed it with his spoon a long stream of juice hit him in the eye, which was very painful."

Meanwhile, the bacon and eggs are getting cold and the marmalade beckons.

"In the end he decided it would be much better if he mixed everything up on the one plate and sat on the tray to eat it." When Judy finds him a little while later he looks up with an "expression of bliss on his face; that part of his face which could be seen behind egg whiskers and toast crumbs".

Breakfast in bed *is* blissful, if a little messy. And plenty of early training in the art of preparing it will ensure that one day the trays are turned and the child who does this is the privileged person to whom it is delivered.

WHAT YOU NEED FOR A
PADDINGTON-STYLE BREAKFAST IN BED

- A tray that won't wobble
- A large napkin
- Plenty of toast, butter, jam and a pot of the best marmalade
- Fried eggs and crispy bacon
- Mug of tea or coffee, or a glass of water, juice or milk
- Half a grapefruit in a bowl and a spoon to gouge and press the fruit for maximum squirting
- A tissue or handkerchief to wipe the grapefruit juice from eyes

NOTE: Leftover bacon can be put in a suitcase and eaten later.

Make a Get-Better Box

MODERN CHILDREN ARE VERY LUCKY TO be spared the misery of measles, mumps and rubella, a truly horrible trio of illnesses. Nevertheless, there are plenty of other illnesses and maladies waiting to strike and turn cheerful, smiley children into miserable, cross and spotty ones like Dorothy Edwards' My Naughty Little Sister when she has measles.

The patient and kind next-door neighbour, Mrs Cocoa Jones, comes to look after her and is prompted to remember the get-better box made by her granny for whoever was poorly and needed cheering up; whenever she found something she thought would amuse a "not-well" child she would put it in her box. And so it became a great treat to borrow the box because although you might know some of its contents, there would always be new things, too. Even Mrs Cocoa Jones finds herself looking forward to seeing it again after many years as she brings it out for the cross, spotty child.

The box looks beautiful and interesting with its covering of various wallpapers from different rooms in different houses, such as Mrs Cocoa Jones' own childhood bedroom, and it contains all sorts of little treasures, often hidden inside tiny, painted boxes within the box. There's a piece of spangle-covered fabric from a dress worn by a real fairy queen in a pantomime, a little string of beads, a tiny doll, a collection of shells, a little paper fan "and in another there was a little laughing clown's face cut out of paper that Mrs Cocoa's granny had stuck there as a surprise", which, sure enough, makes the cross child smile. Then there are picture postcards, some pretty stones (some sparkly, some with holes) a fir cone, pieces of coloured glass, a silver pencil with a magic picture in its handle and a small illustrated book.

Just as Mrs Cocoa Jones expected, "it amused and amused my sister", who takes everything out and sorts and displays and examines and arranges the contents. And rather touchingly, when she's back on her feet, she chalks red spots on her doll and makes her a get-better box with a boot box "so that she could have measles and the get-better box to play with".

Making a get-better box is a lovely thing to do, both for adults in advance of any illness and for children who can be helped to make their own box of treasures. It's very simple, and requires little more than thoughtfulness, imagination and the exercising of a magpie instinct.

CHOOSING AND FILLING A GET-BETTER BOX

➡ Choose a box that will survive frequent handling.

➡ Buy a box or decorate a strong shoe or boot box with wallpaper or wrapping paper.

➡ Collect interesting, unusual items to go inside, and little boxes to go within the big box. Think of a get-better box as a variation on the Christmas stocking theme, but with longer-lasting contents.

SUGGESTIONS FOR CONTENTS

☂ Scraps of fabric, nice buttons, beads, old jewellery, false flowers, feathers, stamps, sequins

☂ Card-making packs from hobby stores and suppliers contain lovely little things – you could include a pack to be used each time the box is needed

- A pack of playing cards
- Unusual little items from foreign countries
- Model cars, planes, toy soldiers, tiny dolls, teddy bears, Russian *matryoshka* dolls, trolls
- Old credit cards, keys, key rings, foreign coins and banknotes
- Photos, postcards, stickers
- Sea glass, shells, unusual stones, fir cones
- Mini-books, mini-packs of colouring pencils, mini-exercise books, tiny pens
- Scrapbook pictures and paper dolls
- Small, amusing toys, for example, a miniature kaleidoscope, wooden puzzles and wind-up toys such as walking, chattering false teeth
- Hawkins Bazaar website and shops are the best places for small toys www.hawkin.com

MORE IDEAS FOR AMUSING POORLY CHILDREN

- Tyke Tyler in *The Turbulent Term of Tyke Tyler* by Gene Kemp enjoys Marvel comics and a bag of sherbet when she is stuck in bed. Second-hand bookshops and charity shops are a great source of old annuals.
- In *The Peppermint Pig* by Nina Bawden, Poll staves off boredom with a scrapbook, a collection of birds' eggs to look at and a large album of family photographs.

Creative Tray Food

CHILDREN (AND MANY ADULTS, TOO) are fascinated and intrigued by food presented on trays, in little boxes and dinky containers, the kind of thing that might be served on a train or in a plane or from a hamper, or perhaps from an exotic, Japanese bento box. There's so much fun to be had in investigating the different parcels or components or compartments, removing the different wrappings and packaging to find out what's inside, and in the possible surprises they may contain. It's also rather lovely to have a selection that has been put together just for you. In fact, it can be incredibly touching, and this is why I like the tray meal that Chunky's mother prepares for him in *The Adventures of Chunky* by Leila Berg.

"Now, whenever Chunky's mother had to leave him to have dinner by himself she always left him a tray that looked interesting. This time there were four parcels on it. One was wrapped in blue paper and stuck down with red, sticky paper. It had a big No. 1 on it, so he opened that first, and found it was three cheese sandwiches made out of cream cheese that his mother made herself. He ate them up and looked for the parcel marked No. 2. This was wrapped in pink tissue paper tied round with golden cord. He opened it, and found a big slice of apple-tart with raisins inside and sugar sprinkled on top.

He ate that up and looked for parcel No. 3. This was a box that was fastened with three blobs of green sealing-wax, and inside there were three large purple plums. He ate those and looked for parcel No. 4. This was wrapped in silver paper with blue circles on it, and stuck down with a sticky gold label that said 'Greetings', and inside was one bar of milk chocolate and four short-cake biscuits."

Isn't that wonderful? Most children must wish they had a mother like Chunky's. I love all the imaginative details of the wrappings, the materials, the colours, the finishing touches, the thoughtfulness, the care. How I wish someone would make a tray of beautifully presented food for me. But until that happens, I suppose the next best thing is for me to make one for someone who would appreciate and enjoy the pleasure of guessing, unwrapping, peeking, pulling out and eating. Which means just about everyone I know.

◌◦ PRACTICAL ◦◌

Creative tray food is also a great lunch-box idea but I really don't think many people could maintain this level of ingenuity and excitement on a regular basis. Treats like this are best saved for a rainy day, for when someone's ill, for a special occasion, for a den, for when you're not there or for a journey.

→ You can use an ordinary kitchen tray and wrap the food in little parcels, or use special small, individual cartons and containers.

→ Becky and Lolo (www.beckyandlolo.co.uk) have a range of fantastic plastic bento boxes (with compartments and boxes within the box) for 'laptop lunches', which are suitable for school and work.

→ The Bag 'n' Box Man (www.bagnboxman.co.uk) sells Chinese-takeaway style cardboard boxes. These could be decorated and personalised with colouring pens and stickers.

→ Or use the classic American-style brown paper food bags

www.lunchboxesetc.co.uk

→ Or Indian tiffin boxes (widely available in Asian supermarkets).

→ Use labels, stickers and tags to prettify and to send little messages.

→ Collect little pieces of ribbon and string, brown parcel paper, wrapping paper and tissue paper or buy in shops such as Paperchase or Ryman, or John Lewis.

→ And sealing wax – now there's a thing. I imagine there are many who would be fascinated by a food parcel with an old-fashioned wax seal. Buy sealing wax from Amazon (www.amazon.co.uk) or eBay (www.ebay.co.uk). It can also be used with some ceremony for sealing letters.

→ Wrap the food in greaseproof paper, aluminium foil or cling film before wrapping it in delicate paper or tissue paper which may spoil when in contact with food – or even colour the food.

Make a Happy Birthday Cake

BIRTHDAYS ARE TAKEN VERY SERIOUSLY in children's books; writers understand their great importance to both their characters and their readers, and treat them with the respect they deserve. And although the children in stories rarely receive huge numbers of presents, many do enjoy quite spectacular, lavish birthday cakes.

Particularly mouth-watering *and* beautiful is Bobbie's birthday cake in *The Railway Children* by E. Nesbit; it's a work of art with an assortment of seasonal flowers lovingly arranged by Peter to depict the railway line. More traditional is Vicky's cake in Arthur Ransome's *Swallows and Amazons*, which is huge and features her name written in pink icing and two large cherries. Poor Joan in *The Naughtiest Girl in the School* by Enid Blyton, whose mother forgets her birthday, saves face by ordering in a ten-shilling cake with eleven candles, lots of colours, sugar flowers and layers of cream that is big enough to feed the entire school. But even her cake is outdone in size and lavishness by the one that staggers John Ruggles in Eve Garnett's *The Family From One End Street* when he accidentally finds himself at a posh birthday party: too big for a mere plate, this cake with chocolate latticework and pale green candles and silver balls sits in splendour on a silver plinth.

All in all, there is no getting away from the fact that when to comes to birthday cakes, size matters and more is more. So here is a recipe for a large sponge cake that can be filled with cream, jam or butter icing, iced with colourful icing and decorated to the hilt.

BIRTHDAY CAKE

Makes one 23 cm cake, enough for 12–16 people

275 g caster sugar

275 g soft butter, plus extra for greasing

4 eggs

275 g self-raising flour

1 teaspoon vanilla extract

2 round (23 cm) cake tins

1. Preheat the oven to 180°C/Gas Mark 4. Grease two 23 cm baking tins with butter and line with baking parchment or greaseproof paper.
2. Cream the sugar and butter in a large mixing bowl until pale and fluffy.
3. Beat the eggs in one at a time (add a teaspoon of flour with each addition if necessary to stop the mix curdling) together with the vanilla extract.
4. Sift in the flour and fold in with a large metal spoon.
5. Divide the mixture evenly between the two cake tins (using scales if you want to be really precise) and bake for 25 minutes until golden and firm. The cake is ready when the top is firm to the touch and a skewer or sharp knife inserted in the centre comes out clean.
6. Leave the cake to cool completely on a wire rack, then turn out of the tins.
7. Fill and ice, and decorate according to the wishes and fantasies of the birthday child.

Buttercream filling

250 g icing sugar

75 g soft butter

Small amount of milk

1. Sift the icing sugar into a bowl and add the butter and 1 tablespoon milk. Mix well with a knife or electric whisk, adding a few more drops of milk if necessary to make butter icing soft and easy to spread.

Icing

300 g icing sugar
Water to mix or the juice of 1–2 lemons
Food colouring (paste rather than liquid is recommended)

1. Sift the icing sugar into a mixing bowl.
2. Gradually add enough water or lemon juice, together with the food colouring, to make a smooth and thick but spreadable icing.
3. Spread the icing on the top of the cake and decorate as desired.

Icing variations

Fondant icing: a soft and glossy icing that is ideal for sponge cakes. It sets well but doesn't turn rock hard. It's very easy to make with the commercial fondant icing sugar that is now widely available.

Ready-to-roll icing: perfect for a thick, firm, smooth cake covering that be can be coloured with food colouring paste if desired, then decorated and embellished. It gives great results for very little effort.

Writing and messages: either make your own royal icing (the easiest way is to use royal icing sugar to which you just add water) and use a simple piping kit, or buy the ready-to-write tubes of coloured icing.

And So to Bed…

ONE OF THE HIGHLIGHTS OF STAYING in a hotel is finding a chocolate placed anonymously on the pillow before you go to bed. Better still, though, is the discovery of a secret delivery of freshly made biscuits on the bedside table; it's as if a little fairy or elf has visited and left a token, a little gift, a wish for a good night's sleep.

Gifts that can be given and received at bedtime are delightful. Hot-water bottles, storybooks, warm drinks, extra pillows and blankets, patchwork quilts and soft teddy bears are all very much appreciated, but when I read *The Little White Horse* by Elizabeth Goudge I realised I had never fully explored the true extent of bedtime luxuries.

Maria arrives at Moonacre at night and is shown to her new bedroom in which every detail of decor and comfort has been considered. There are candles in silver candlesticks, a sheepskin rug by the four-poster bed with pale blue silk curtains, pillows filled with lavender, and a feather mattress, an exquisite patchwork quilt, a little mirror and a large fire that fills the room with the fragrance of pine cones and apple wood. And above the fireplace she finds a "blue wooden box filled with dainty biscuits with sugar flowers on them, in case she should feel hungry between meals".

As if this wasn't enough, when she comes to bed after supper she discovers that someone, she knows not who (it's Marmaduke Scarlet), has been in the room, stoked the fire, warmed the bed with a warming pan, and left a glass of milk by the biscuits.

"Well, whoever it was, it gave her a lovely warm happy feeling to find herself so cared for. As she undressed, she sipped her milk, and it was warm and sweet just as she liked it. And the sugar biscuit that she ate with it, a long-shoed one decorated with a green shamrock, was delicious too."

Oh, my. Biscuits topped with lucky green shamrocks certainly make hotel chocolates pale into insignificance.

PILLOW BISCUITS

Although they may sound fiddly and faffy, 'pillow biscuits' are easy to make and are the perfect bedtime gift for someone tiptoeing about in a dressing gown to leave on a pillow. They can be cut into any shape, iced and decorated to suit the recipient, and could even spell out goodnight messages.

This recipe gives a dough that is suitable for children to work with – and the results will still taste good. It's not too buttery or soft and can withstand a reasonable amount of rolling, handling and cutting before baking. Making these biscuits is a lovely, absorbing activity for children of all ages and can easily fill a wet winter's afternoon.

NOTE: Allow an hour or two between making the dough and rolling, cutting etc as the dough needs time to 'rest' in the fridge.

Makes 40–50 biscuits depending on cutter size and shape

200 g butter

200 g caster sugar

1 egg

400 g plain flour, plus extra for dusting

Flavouring (optional): grated orange or lemon peel, or 1 teaspoon vanilla extract, or

   1 teaspoon of caraway seeds (if making Katy's spendiferous loft feast caraway cookies)

1. In a large mixing bowl cream the butter and sugar until pale and fluffy.
2. Beat in the egg until the mix is well combined.
3. Sift in the flour, add flavouring if using, and mix with a wooden spoon or your hand to make a firm dough.
4. Divide the dough into two balls, flatten them slightly, wrap in cling film and put in the fridge to chill.
5. When you are ready to roll and bake, preheat the oven to 180°C/Gas Mark
4. Line two baking trays with baking parchment or greaseproof paper.
6. On a lightly floured work surface, roll out one of the balls to a thickness of approximately 5 mm. Cut into shapes with cookie cutters and transfer carefully to a baking tray.
7. Bake for 8–12 minutes, depending on the size of your biscuits, until pale gold. Do not allow them to brown. Leave to cool on a wire rack while you take the next ball of dough out of the fridge and get on with the next batch of biscuits.
8. Decorate the biscuits when they are cold.

Decorations

➡ Icing made with 300g icing sugar and enough water or lemon juice to make a smooth, spreadable covering. Colour as desired.

➡ Sugar flowers, sprinkles, crystallised petals, silver balls, sweets.

MORE WAYS TO CREATE A LOVELY, WARM, HAPPY, CARED-FOR FEELING

☂ Leave little letters, cards, messages or hand-drawn pictures on or under pillows.

☂ Set up a night-time post office (see page 267).

10 suggestions for bedtime reading

1. Fairy tales, especially the famous ones with lots of night-time goings-on such as 'The Princess and the Pea' and 'The Twelve Dancing Princesses'

2. **_Goodnight Moon_, Margaret Wise Brown (with lovely illustrations by Clement Hurd so that you can enjoy the ritual of saying goodnight to everything in the bedroom)**

3. _Peter Pan_, J.M. Barrie (what happens after Peter sneaks into the nursery to listen to Mrs Darling's bedtime stories)

4. _Five go to Smuggler's Top_, Enid Blyton (action-packed, after lights-out adventure story with the heroes dressed in pyjamas)

5. **_A Little Princess_, Frances Hodgson Burnett (heart-rending riches-to-rags and back again story, to encourage the counting of blessings rather than sheep)**

6. _Goodnight Mr Tom_, Michelle Magorian (a young evacuee overcomes war and night-time traumas with the help of curmudgeonly but kind Mr Tom)

7. _Charlie and the Chocolate Factory_, Roald Dahl (to give you sweet dreams)

8. **_Alice's Adventures in Wonderland_, Lewis Carroll (was it all a dream?)**

9. Poems (perfect for bedtime)

10. Your own, made-up stories (as conventional or as wild as you like – children will love them)

More Bookish Adventures

ALTHOUGH THERE ARE PLENTY OF PRACTICAL ideas and suggestions in the main chapters, this section contains recommendations for further reading for each topic. It's a mix of great works of fiction for children and the best practical guides, handbooks and 'how-to' books currently available.

SECRETS AND SPIES

Invaluable Guides
The Detective's Handbook, Colin King (Usborne, 2008)
The Spy's Guidebook, Colin King (Usborne, 2008)

Ripping Reads
Sherlock Holmes stories by Arthur Conan Doyle
Famous Five, Secret Seven and Five Find-Outer stories by Enid Blyton
The 'Lone Pine' books by Malcolm Saville

As well as the classic Biggles books by W.E. Johns, there are some tremendous contemporary writers who exploit the world of spies, codes, undercover agents and secret services. The best are: Chris Ryan's Code Red books, Anthony Horowitz's Alex Rider books, Robert Muchamore's Cherub books and Charlie Higson's Young James Bond books

SCIENTIFIC THINKING
Invaluable Guides
Oxford Astronomy, Jacqueline Mitton and Simon Mitton (Young Oxford Books, 1996)
Philip's Pocket Star Atlas, John Cox (Philip's, 2005)

IN THE KITCHEN
Invaluable Guides
The River Cottage Family Cookbook, Hugh Fearnley-Whittingstall and Fizz Carr (Hodder & Stoughton, 2005)
Easy Peasy, Mary Contini and Pru Irvine (Ebury Press, 1999)

Ripping Reads
George's Marvellous Medicine, Roald Dahl (Puffin) is an absolute must for everyone who likes making mixtures; children will relish every detail of the mindbogglingly awful mixtures, or medicine, made by George to 'cure' his hateful gran.

MAKING STUFF
Invaluable Guides
Crazy Patchwork, Janet Haigh (Collins & Brown, 1998)
Crafting with Kids, Catherine Worham (Ryland, Peters and Small, 2006)

Kids Knitting, Melanie Falick (Artisan, 1998) – By far the best book on knitting with children. It covers everything from winding a ball to making your own knitting needles, from basic stitches to knitting with colour

First Knits, Luise Roberts and Kate Haxell (Collins & Brown, 2005) – Suitable for older beginners (ten plus)

SUMMER DAYS
Invaluable Guides
Food for Free, Richard Mabey (Collins, 2007) – The classic reference work on gathering and foraging

TREES
Invaluable Guides
Gardening with Kids, Martyn Cox and Catherine Woram (Ryland, Peters & Small, 2008)

David Stiles is the tree-house builder's guru. For inspiration and practical advice see www.stilesdesigns.com

RIPPING GAMES
Invaluable Guides
Chambers Card Games, Peter Arnold (Chambers Harrap, 2007)

Kiss Chase and Conkers: The Games We Played, Caroline Sanderson (Harrap Cahmbers, 2008) – A wonderfully nostalgic reminder of the many traditional games played by children in the twentieth century, complete with how-to-play instructions and rules

DREAMS AND SCHEMES
Invaluable Guides
Planted Junk, Adam Caplin (Ryland Peters and Small, 2001) – Full of excellent and visually stunning ideas for growing plants in recycled containers.

Grow Your Own Cut Flowers, Sarah Raven (BBC, 2002) – Very useful section on hardy annuals.

How to Draw Horses, Lucy Smith et al (Usborne Books, 2003)

The Kingfisher Illustrated Horse and Pony Encyclopedia, Sandy Ransford (2004)

Ripping Reads
There is no shortage of pony stories and there are several writers who have written dozens of pony books which satisfy the desire to own a pony vicariously. Look for more books by Monica Edwards or any of the following: *Black Beauty*, Anna Sewell, *National Velvet*, Enid Bagnold (and the classic 1944 film version starring Elizabeth Taylor), *Jill's Gymkhana*, Ruby Ferguson or any of the dozens of books by the Pullein-Thompson sisters

RED LETTER DAYS
Invaluable Guides
Adrian Fisher is the world's leading maze designer. Look at www.adrianfisherdesign.co.uk for details of the mazes he has designed in the United Kingdom and all over the world. The site has updates on the best maize mazes each summer. His books are also excellent

AMAZING ADVENTURES
Invaluable Guides
Waterlog: A Swimmer's Journey Through Britain, Roger Deakin (Vintage, 2000) – The book that inspired the renewal of interest in outdoor swimming and

something of a classic. It is highly recommended for anyone who enjoys or is interested in swimming outdoors. Includes a chapter on coracles.

Wild Swim: River Lake, Lido and Sea: the Best Places to Swim Outdoors in Britain, Kate Rew and Dominick Tyler (Guardian, 2008)

Ripping Reads

Inspire young sailors with some classic boating and sailing tales such as the Swallows and Amazons series by Arthur Ransome

The Minnow on the Say, Philippa Pearce

My Family and Other Animals, Gerald Durrell

The Wind in the Willows, Kenneth Grahame

Treasure Island, Robert Louis Stevenson

WINTER DAYS

Ripping Reads

The Snow Queen, Hans Christian Anderson

The Lion, the Witch and the Wardrobe, C.S. Lewis

TREATS AND REMEDIES

Ripping Reads

You'll find more lovely and creative trays of food in:

A Bear Called Paddington, Michael Bond

Dancing Shoes, Noel Streatfeild

Wish for a Pony, Monica Edwards

Acknowledgements

I WOULD LIKE TO THANK ALL THE TEAM at Hodder & Stoughton, in particular Nicky Ross for spotting the potential of the book's central idea, Zelda Turner for her clear thinking and fine editorial skills, and Sarah Hammond for her marvellous organisational capabilities and invaluable work on permissions and schedules. Marissa Cox also deserves a huge thank-you, as does Alice Laurent who created the wonderful design for the cover and text, and commissioned the delightful original illustrations by Polly Webb-Wilson. Thanks also to Janette Revill for her beautiful design of the book's contents.

Jane Graham Maw and Jennifer Christie of Graham Maw Christie, my agent, have once again been wonderfully reliable and helpful and I thank them for their support.

I'd like to thank my mum for encouraging me to do the things I'd read about in books and for the visits to the castles, and my brother Matthew and my sister Kate for the unforgettably funny shows they put on for our entertainment. I'm also grateful to Kate for organising marvellous Easter egg hunts for my children. The book also draws on the many good times I shared with my late brother, Roger, who was always ready with a penknife, a box of matches and a pack of cards to go off on a camping- or den-building adventure.

Throughout the writing of this book I have been sustained by the encouragement, enthusiasm and good humour of my husband Simon and our children Tom, Alice and Phoebe, and by the memories of the magical times we have had together doing so many of the things described here. I consider myself very fortunate to have had you there every time I emerged from the literary world back into the real one. Thank you.

TEXT ACKNOWLEDGEMENTS

Nina Bawden, *The Peppermint Pig* (Puffin, 1997), copyright © Nina Bawden. Reproduced by permission of Penguin Books Ltd; Leila Berg, *The Adventures of Chunky* (Oxford University Press, 1958); Enid Blyton, *The Mystery of the Secret Room* (Egmont, 2002); Enid Blyton, *Five Fall Into Adventure* (Hodder & Stoughton, 1997); Enid Blyton, *The Rat-a-Tat Mystery* (Collins, 1956), © Chorion Rights Limited. All rights reserved; Enid Blyton, *Well Done, Secret Seven* (Hodder Children's Books, 2006); Enid Blyton, *Five Go to Smugglers Top* (Hodder & Stoughton, 1997); Enid Blyton, *Five Run Away Together* (Hodder & Stoughton, 1997), © 1944 Chorion Rights Limited. All rights reserved; Michael Bond, *A Bear Called Paddington* (HarperCollins, 2003); Mary Grant Bruce, *A Little Bush Maid* (Ward, Lock, 1910). Reproduced by permission of Curtis Brown Literary Agents, Australia; Anthony Buckeridge, *Jennings Goes to School* (Penguin, 1965); Anthony Buckeridge, *Jennings Follows a Clue* (Collins, 1958); Betsy Byars, *The Midnight Fox* (Puffin, 1998); Richmal Crompton, *William Again* (Macmillan Children's Books, 2005); Roald Dahl, *Danny the Champion of the World* (Puffin, 2001). Reproduced by permission of David Higham Associates; Gerald Durrell, *My Family and Other Animals* (Penguin Books, 1959); Dorothy Edwards, *My Naughty Little Sister's Friends* (Egmont, 2007); Dorothy Edwards, *My Naughty Little Sister* (Egmont, 2002), text © Dorothy Edwards 1962; Elizabeth Enright, *The Saturdays* (Puffin, 1971). Elizabeth Enright, *Thimble Summer* (Puffin, 1972); Antonia Fraser, *Autumn Term* (Faber, 2000). Reproduced by permission of the publisher; Eve Garnett, *The Family from One End Street* (Puffin Modern Classics, 1942), text and illustrations 1937 by Eve Garnett. Introduction © copyright Julia Eccleshare, 2004. Reproduced by permission of Penguin Books Ltd; Elizabeth Goudge, *Linnets and Valerians* (Hodder & Stoughton, 1982); Elizabeth Goudge, *The Little White Horse* (Lion Hudson, 1988); Shirley Hughes, *Alfie's Feet* (Red Fox, 2004). Reproduced by permission of The Random House Group Ltd; Madeleine L'Engle, *A Wrinkle in Time* (Puffin, 1967), copyright © Madeleine L'Engle, 1962. Reproduced by permission of Penguin Books Ltd;

Astrid Lindgren, *Pippi Longstocking* (Oxford University Press, 2007); Maud Hart Lovelace, *Betsy-Tacy and Tib* (HarperTrophy, 2000); John Masefield, *The Box of Delights* (Egmont, 2003). Reproduced by permission of The Society of Authors as the literary representative of the Estate of John Masefield; Magdalen Nabb, *Josie Smith in Spring* (HarperCollins, 2000); Mary Norton, *The Borrowers* (Puffin, 2003); Philippa Pearce, *Tom's Midnight Garden* (Puffin, 2003); Arthur Ransome, *Winter Holiday* (Red Fox, 2001). Reproduced by permission of The Random House Group Ltd; Arthur Ransome, *Swallows and Amazons* (Red Fox, 2001). Reproduced by permission of The Random House Group Ltd; Noel Streatfeild, *Ballet Shoes* (Puffin, 2004); Barbara Euphan Todd, *Worzel Gummidge* (Puffin, 1950); E.B. White, *Charlotte's Web* (Puffin, 1993), copyright © 1952 by J. White. Reproduced by permission of Penguin Books Ltd; Laura Ingalls Wilder, *Little House in the Big Woods* (Egmont, 2000).

PICTURE ACKNOWLEDGEMENTS

Leila Berg, *The Adventures of Chunky* (Oxford University Press, 1958), illustration by George Downs: 287. Enid Blyton, *Five Go to Smuggler's Top* (Hodder and Stoughton, 1997), illustration by Eileen Soper: 15. Enid Blyton, *Five on a Hike Together* (Hodder & Stoughton, 1997), illustration by Eileen Soper: 215. Enid Blyton, *Five on a Treasure Island* (Hodder and Stoughton, 1997) © 1997, illustration by Eileen Soper: 189. Enid Blyton, *Five on Kirrin Island Again* (Hodder & Stoughton, 1997) © 1997, illustration by Eileen Soper: 5. Enid Blyton, *The Secret of Spiggy Holes* (Basil Blackwell, 1940), illustrations by E.H. Davie, reproduced by permission of the publisher: iv, 223, 297. Enid Blyton, *Well Done, Secret Seven* (Hodder, 1996), illustration by George Brook: 89. Michael Bond, *A Bear Called Paddington* (HarperCollins, 2003) © 2003, illustrated by Peggy Fortnum: 281. Joyce Lankester Brisley, *The Adventures of Milly-Molly-Mandy* (Macmillan Children's Books, 1992), illustrations by Joyce Lankester Brisley: 47, 54, 61, 74, 217, 227, 263, 271. Richmal Crompton, *William Again* (Macmillan Children's Books, 2005), illustrated by Thomas Henry: 123. Roald Dahl, *Danny the Champion of the World* (Puffin, 2001), illustration by Quentin Blake: 225. Dorothy Edwards, *My Naughty Little Sister* (Egmont, 2002), illustration by Shirley Hughes: 59. Dorothy Edwards, *My Naughty Little Sister's Friends* (Egmont, 2007), illustration by Shirley Hughes: 283. Elizabeth Enright, *Thimble Summer* (Puffin, 1972), illustrations by Elizabeth Enright: 11, 159. Elizabeth Enright, *The Saturdays* (Puffin, 1971), illustration by Elizabeth Enright: 181. Eve Garnett, *The Family from One End Street* (Puffin Modern Classics, 1942), illustration by Eve Garnett, reproduced by permission of Penguin Books Ltd: 191. Shirley Hughes, *Alfie's Feet* (Red Fox, 2004), illustration by Shirley Hughes, reproduced by permission of The Random House Group Ltd: 175. Astrid Lindgren, *Pippi Longstocking* (Oxford University Press, 2004), illustration by Tony Ross: 94. Maud Hart Lovelace, *Betsy-Tacy and Tib* (HarperTrophy, 2000), illustrations by Lois Lenski: 39, 274. A. A. Milne, *The House at Pooh Corner* (Egmont, 2004), illustrations by E.H. Shepard: 111. Magdalen Nabb, *Josie Smith in Spring* (HarperCollins, 2000), illustration by Karen Donnelly: 131. Mary Norton, *The Borrowers* (Puffin, 2003), illustration by Sian Bailey: 51. Philippa Pearce, *Tom's Midnight Garden* (Puffin, 2003), illustration by Barbara Brown: 1, 162, 237. Arthur Ransome, *Winter Holiday* (Red Fox, 2001), illustration by Arthur Ransome: 21. Noel Streatfeild, *Ballet Shoes* (Puffin, 2004), illustrations by Ruth Gervis: 57, 199. Barbara Euphan Todd, *Worzel Gummidge* (Puffin, 1950), illustration by John Harwood: 155. E.B. White, *Charlotte's Web* (Puffin, 1993), illustrations by Garth Williams: 81, 213. Laura Ingalls Wilder, *Little House in the Big Woods* (Egmont, 2000), illustration by Garth Williams: 233.

Illustrations on pages 29, 33, 66, 78-9, 91, 96, 141-3, 151, 194, 234-5 by Polly Webb-Wilson.

Every reasonable effort has been made to contact the copyright holders, but if there are any errors or omissions, Hodder & Stoughton will be pleased to insert the appropriate acknowledgement in any subsequent printing of this publication.

Index